ENEMY ANCESTORS

ENEMY ANCESTORS

The
Anasazi
World
with a Guide
to Sites

Text by

Gary Matlock

Photographs by

Scott Warren

 NORTHLAND PUBLISHING

FRONTISPIECE

Pictograph handprints in a southeastern Utah canyon; handprints were a common Anasazi motif.

Design by Richard Hendel
Edited by Rose Houk
Illustrations by David Jenney
Typesetting by Marathon Typography Service, Inc.

Text copyright © 1988 by Gary Matlock

Photographs copyright © 1988 by Scott Warren

FIRST EDITION

Second Printing 1991

All Rights Reserved

ISBN 0-87358-458-9 softcover

Library of Congress Catalog Card Number

87-42824

Printed and Bound in Japan by Dai Nippon

3-88/7.5M/0023

2-91/5M/0336

Library of Congress

Cataloging-in-Publication Data

Matlock, Gary, 1941–

    Enemy ancestors.

    Bibliography

    Includes index.

    1. Pueblo Indians—Antiquities. 2. Indians of North America—Southwest, New—Antiquities. 3. Southwest, New—Description and travel—1981– —Guide-books. 4. Southwest, New—Antiquities. I. Title.

E99.P9M357   1987   979.01   87-42824

ISBN 0-87358-458-9 (pbk.)

TO JAN, TO BETH

and to the preservation of

the nation's irreplaceable antiquities

Contents

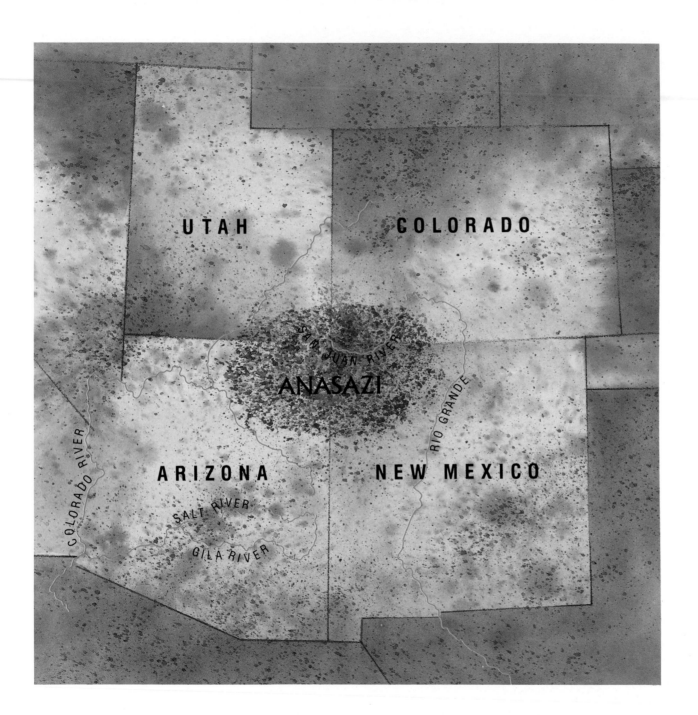

Preface

In 1888 a southwestern Colorado cowboy named Richard Wetherill rode horseback through the dense pinyon pine forest atop the Mesa Verde searching for cows. It was December, the ground was covered with snow, and the air was crisp and cold. He emerged from the pinyon at the edge of a deep sandstone canyon, and looking across, saw an astonishing sight—the adobe and stone walls of the largest intact prehistoric community in the United States. Richard was never to be much of a cowboy again. Riding to the head of the canyon, he spent most of the day climbing in the centuries-old village which was filled with pottery, basketry, stone and bone tools, and literally thousands of other artifacts and remains of the Anasazi Indians who built and occupied the ruin in the thirteenth century.

The people who occupied the Four Corners area of the American Southwest during the era between roughly 200 B.C. and A.D. 1300 were designated "Anasazi" by archaeologist Alfred V. Kidder in 1936. The word is from the Navajo language and has been construed to mean "the old ones," or "the ancient ones." A more recent interpretation of its meaning is "enemy ancestors," reasonable in view of the Navajos' cultural aversion to places where deaths have occurred. The imposing and deserted multi-roomed Anasazi structures must have seemed like ghost towns to the Navajos who began drifting into the area in the sixteenth century. Three centuries later, Wetherill was no doubt stunned by the sight.

For the rest of his life, another twenty-two years, Richard Wetherill searched hundreds of canyons and mesas in Colorado, New Mexico, Utah, and Arizona for additional ruined villages. The large ruin that he had found on the Mesa Verde is today called Cliff Palace, the largest and best-known of the thousands of prehistoric sites in America. Most of Mesa Verde is now a national park, visited each year by nearly a half million people from the United States and throughout the world.

Besides the large cliff ruins of Mesa Verde, Richard Wetherill was responsible for discovering, and to a large degree, familiarizing the rest of the world with many of the major sites in the Southwest, including large ruins now part of other parks and monuments, such as Tsegi Canyon in northeastern Arizona, the enormous prehistoric cities in Chaco Canyon, and hundreds of sites in southeastern Utah.

Cliff Palace and many of the other large ruins of the Southwest were discovered only about a hundred years ago —not a long time in the eyes of an archaeologist. A few years ago, we thought that all the large spectacular Anasazi ruins had been found. However, in 1986, the School of American Research in Santa Fe, New Mexico, announced the discovery of several sites, including a thirty-room cliff dwelling

"All-American Man,"
a famous pictograph
in the Needles Dis-
trict of Canyonlands
National Park, Utah.

*Stabilized walls of the
Chimney Rock site
in the San Juan Na-
tional Forest of south-
ern Colorado.*

The Knife's Edge in Mesa Verde National Park, Colorado; mesas and canyons of the Four Corners area were the home of the Anasazi.

Shiprock, a prominent New Mexico landmark, may have held special meaning for the Anasazi, as it does for modern-day cultures.

*Spider Rock, Canyon
de Chelly, Arizona.*

ways we view and use the land far differently. We have, for example, superimposed arbitrary state boundaries over natural ones. These complicate our understanding of the very different political and cultural boundaries of the Anasazi which were probably more reflective of the natural environments. While we have developed an unparalleled knowledge through science and technology of our universe and its systems and functions, we have long lost an understanding of the communities of plants and animals, minerals, water, and dozens of other resources important to the Anasazi. And no doubt, because of our scientifically colored view, we perceive the land's beauty, its dimensions, and its value differently.

But like the Anasazi, we can still wander the Four Corners more or less freely. True, private land ownership and certain government and tribal restrictions apply. But relative to the rest of the United States and, in fact, much of the world, the Anasazi Southwest is largely open and available to us to go in most any direction we choose and by whatever means of transport. From the high mountains administered by the U.S. Forest Service to the pinyon-covered mesas and desert sandstone canyons managed largely by the U.S. Bureau of Land Management, there are literally hundreds of unpopulated square miles of enormously varied landscape for the hiker, back-road driver, river-boater, or other adventurer to explore

—enough open land to occupy a person for at least a lifetime.

Scattered over this entire area are thousands of Anasazi sites. It is rare to walk for more than a mile along a mesa or up a canyon without encountering an Anasazi ruin littered with broken pottery and stone chips and tumbled masonry walls.

Geology

The Anasazi Southwest consists of relatively thin soils over much thicker horizontal rock layers. The formations are sediments—sands, clays, limes, and other basic materials —deposited by ancient eroding mountains and inland seas. Erosion formed, and is still forming, arroyos, river valleys, mesas, and canyons. Tectonic or volcanic processes also play a part in forming mountain ranges, dikes, and isolated rock forms such as Shiprock in New Mexico and Agathla in Arizona.

All of these land forms are a part of a great geologic province—the Colorado Plateau—something of a geologic anomaly. The plateau is some 130,000 square miles of relatively flat, elevated land. Its northern edge follows the base of the Rocky Mountains in Colorado, extending south to Flagstaff and the Mogollon Rim in Arizona, east to the Rio Grande Valley in New Mexico, and west to the Basin and Range of Utah. Much of the Plateau consists primar-

ily of beds of sandstones and clays with occasional conglomerates and thick layers of limestones. At least a score or more of these geological formations are exposed in the Four Corners, with colorful names and colorful materials such as the uranium-bearing Chinle formation, thick white or red Navajo Sandstone, gray Mancos Shale, sheer-walled Entrada Sandstone, and fossil-rich Morrison formation. These formations provided some of the most basic materials for the Anasazi—sandstone for house construction; clay for pottery; fine-grained chert, flint, and chalcedony for stone tools; and the rarer stones and clays for paints in ceremonies and fetishes.

The red clay soils of decomposing Dakota Sandstone, Mancos Shale, and the airborne red sands from the deserts to the west, formed the Anasazi farm lands in southwestern Colorado and southeastern Utah. In these rich soils were grown corn, beans, and squash, and, where the climate would allow, cotton.

The porous sandstone beds are also groundwater reservoirs. Seeps and springs occur regularly at the base of sandstone formations where they meet shales or limestones. Sheets of water run off the slickrock after thunderous summer rainstorms, water that the Anasazi controlled and directed onto fields situated below.

These resources also constrained and defined the nature of Anasazi technol-

*Wild squash grows at
the base of this Can-
yonlands National
Park dwelling.*

ogy and, therefore, the elements and forms of the culture itself. For example, some of the differences in masonry types between the various branches of the Four Corners Anasazi may be due to the nature of the sandstones available to them for building. In the Northern San Juan Anasazi culture area of Colorado and Utah, the Dakota and the Cliff House sandstones were the rock used for the building stones for houses, villages, and kivas. These relatively hard sandstones lend themselves to being worked by chipping, and finer pecking and grinding of the surface. They form the beautiful, nearly perfectly square or rectangular stone blocks used in Mesa Verde construction. On the other hand, the material available to the Kayenta Anasazi was Navajo Sandstone and other much softer sandstones that generally do not lend themselves to such fine work because they tend to break or split. As a result, Kayenta masonry shows crudely shaped fragments of rock with little refining or working of the basic stone.

At Chaco Canyon in northern New Mexico, the Anasazi used stone from thin beds in the Cliff House Sandstone, constructing extremely fine and beautiful walls of banded small stone masonry for which the Chaco are well known. Of course, materials alone do not totally determine the nature and technology of any given people, Anasazi or otherwise, but they do influence that technology.

A similar situation may exist with Anasazi ceramic technology. Different clays produce pottery with varying degrees of strength, thinness, color, cracking, and other characteristics that define a given pottery style. Mesa Verde Black on White which has a smooth creamy surface may have been the result of a particular clay found in the Mancos Shale, for example. The nature of the clay used will often limit and define the nature of the final product to some degree. This may explain why neither specific Chaco or Mesa Verde ceramic styles has been found in the Rio Grande Valley where the Anasazi presumably migrated when they abandoned the Four Corners. The clay sources in the Rio Grande Valley may not have permitted the strict duplication of those styles.

The character of the geological formations also provides a setting for the spectacular cliff dwellings at Mesa Verde and other canyon locations in the Four Corners. The relative hardness of the sandstone and erosion processes form sheer sandstone cliffs and nearly vertical canyon walls. The alcoves or shallow caves, formed by the same hydrologic process that created springs, became the predominant village locations in the thirteenth century for those Four Corners Anasazi who remained.

Climate

The climate of the Southwest—rainfall, temperature, humidity, and other characteristics—is another key environmental factor in the development of Anasazi culture. At first glance, it seems unlikely that this arid or semiarid region could have supported a large farming population for nearly 1,300 years. But the same marginal climate that wooed the earliest Anasazi, the Basketmakers, into farming also provided at least adequate conditions for later, more intensive horticulture and agriculture. Slight changes in rainfall likely influenced directly the agricultural productivity of the Anasazi and, as a result, many other aspects of their lives such as the tendency to abandon some locations regularly and move to others. This rainfall dependancy must also have affected population growth and village size. In the end, probably many of the kiva rituals and other aspects of Anasazi religion are closely associated with the fickle southwestern climate.

Reconstructing past climates, or paleoclimates as they are known, has become a major preoccupation of archaeologists and kindred scientists such as botanists, foresters, tree-ring analysts, pollen experts, geologists, snail specialists, and others. Changes in yearly rainfall, temperature, timberline in the mountains, plant communities, soils, river runoff, and other climatic

*A well-preserved site
in a southeastern
Utah canyon.*

functions have been charted with a fairly high degree of accuracy.

The result of this research has been a beginning in understanding the effects on the Anasazi of even small changes in climate. For example, the largest villages, greatest population growth, and development of specialized kivas occurred during a period of ample moisture and an adequate growing season throughout much of the Southwest. A time of reduced moisture and lower temperatures followed, during which much of the Anasazi population moved to lower elevations. The end of the highly complex Chaco trading system between A.D. 1130 and 1180 was also a period of extended dryness in the Four Corners. Climatic change may not be the only reason the system ceased to function, but it seems to be one of them.

The amazing summer ceremonials of the Pueblos today—corn dances, kachina dances, and the Hopi Snake Dance—are all closely associated with the unpredictable southwestern summer rains. Many of these "modern" rituals were developed to some degree by the Anasazi in response to anxiety over late-summer rain for their crops.

The interplay between geology, land forms, and climate is also responsible for the existence of microenvironments that were so crucial to Anasazi agriculture. For example, some of the extensive flat mesas such as those at Mesa Verde and similar ones that were major agricultural areas for the Anasazi, are tilted to the south or southeast. The result is that the entire mesa acts like a solar collector, increasing the effective average temperature and the growing season with no particular loss of rainfall or available moisture.

Plants and Animals

Despite increasing reliance upon farming, the Anasazi never completely stopped gathering plants and hunting animals. In fact, in times of environmental stress such as low rainfall, a shorter growing season, or perhaps too many mouths to feed, the Anasazi consistently increased their use of these wild resources. It is also certain that the amazing success of the Anasazi and their modern Pueblo descendants—that is, the rich cultural lifeway they sustained for more than 2,000 years to date—was in large part due to their ability both to farm and to hunt and gather. There may, in fact, be a lesson or two for contemporary southwestern people in this balance.

The mesas of southwestern Colorado, southeastern Utah, and the higher mesas of northeastern Arizona are densely covered with a forest of pinyon pine and juniper. This extensive forest is found from 5,500 or 6,000 feet up to 7,500—about the altitudinal band where most Northern San Juan Anasazi lived. In other places great open areas were covered with six-foot-high sagebrush both before and after the Anasazi occupation and before the present day intensive Anglo occupation. Sage would probably be more apparent today except that many farming areas are in the Great Sage Plains of the Southwest. These two plant communities are the predominant vegetation of the Southwest.

In addition to the pinyon-juniper forests and sagebrush flats, plants include many desert-adapted shrubs, grasses, flowers, yuccas, and others. Shrubs include mountain mahogany, service berry, cliff rose, fendler bush and others. Several dozen prominent species of flowering cactus are common as well as a variety of colorful plants including bee weed, globe mallow, composites such as daisies and sunflowers, and the ever-present penstemon and scarlet gilia. Along streams and around desert springs, small oasis-like microenvironments support cottonwoods, hackberry, mosses, ivy, and other riparian plants.

In the high country Douglas fir, ponderosa pine, and spruce forests are also very much a part of southwestern plant communities. And, in the lower elevations and in canyon bottoms there are full desert conditions, with no trees and only low-growing shrubs, cactus, and grasses.

Of the multitude of plants used by

the Anasazi, some have been identified as having been more important than others. The major food plants were the Rocky Mountain bee plant, used also for the black paint on some ceramics; a common but not frequently recognized plant called pigweed, which produced a large number of usable seeds; another "weed," goosefoot, also a major seed producer; and, finally, the better known and most beautiful of all southwestern grasses, the distinctive rice grass. These plants and many others provided an extensive and important food resource used either by themselves or as supplements to cultivated crops.

Another major plant was the yucca. It provided the primary fiber for sandals, ropes, nets, and a variety of cordage. The pods and seeds were eaten and the roots made an excellent soap for, among other things, washing hair. Modern Zunis insist that yucca soap prevents baldness, which, although probably genetic, is indeed a rare occurrence among Pueblo and other Indians.

The list of plant resources found in the Four Corners or those used by the Anasazi could be expanded at great length based on the amount of archaeological data available today. Though it may appear barren, the Four Corners area is rich in plant resources. Some of them, such as rice grasses which are favored by cattle over most other grass species, are hard to find today except in national parks and other protected locations. Many others are still available and certainly usable.

Like plants, animals too were important to the Anasazi. For the most part, the animal communities are also much the same today as they were during Anasazi times. Large mammals in the pinyon-juniper zone include deer, antelope, and desert bighorn sheep. Based on bones recovered from trash deposits or "middens" at Anasazi sites, these were frequently used for food. The bones of elk and other high-mountain animals are found less frequently. However, because these animals were farther away they may have been more completely butchered at the kill site, thus fewer bones would be returned to the homesite and would be less likely to be found in Anasazi middens.

Probably the single most important meat source for the Anasazi were the several species of rabbits. Rabbit bones, fur, and specialized tools such as yucca nets, snares, and a distinctive "rabbit stick" still used by the Pueblo today are common in Anasazi sites. Again, however, the archaeological record may be misleading because rabbits are easily returned and butchered at the site.

Finally, although rarely found today, the turkey was not only an important food resource, but was also apparently domesticated and its feathers used for blankets and other purposes. Turkey pens have been found in a number of sites, including some in Grand Gulch in southeastern Utah.

Though we commonly think of the Anasazi inhabiting the lower and drier parts of the Southwest, in fact, they lived in and used nearly all the environments of the region. The mountains were sources of summer food, raw materials such as chert and obsidian, wood, and medicinal and ritual resources; and they offered a break from the more monotonous mesas and plateaus. The primary village sites are found in the denser pinyon forests on plateaus and mesa tops or in large, open valley bottoms. For the most part, the better-known spectacular canyon cliff sites were only occupied late in the long sequence of Anasazi settlement of the Four Corners, when the population was much reduced.

However, population density in different environments varied from one time to another, as did the concentration of population in one place or another. Intensive occupation in the lower, drier regions of Chaco Canyon, for example, did not begin until about A.D. 900, while the pinyon forest area around Black Mesa in Arizona and the ponderosa-covered valleys near Durango, Colorado, were occupied before the birth of Christ. Utilization of different environments changed over time and one of the most consistent characteristics of the Anasazi was their tendency to abandon certain areas, move to new ones, only to reoccupy old areas a century or two later. Much of this relocation was probably in response to slight changes in rainfall or other environmental conditions that affected agricultural production.

Overall, population density through-

*Interior of Pueblo
Bonito, Chaco
Culture National
Historic Park, New
Mexico.*

out most of the Anasazi Southwest through time was low. But periodically certain areas, such as Chaco Canyon or the Tsegi Canyon area, appeared to flourish. Only in the Mesa Verde region in southwestern Colorado did occupation and consistent development seem to occur throughout the first thirteen centuries. But even in the Mesa Verde region frequent minor relocations were common.

In the end, it was probably this same inconsistent environment that both permitted agriculture for some thirteen centuries but was also ultimately responsible for the short migration of the Anasazi from the Four Corners to more southern regions. It may also have been the primary limiting factor that prevented the Anasazi from leaving the Formative or farming level of cultural development to achieve the more complex state or urban levels found in Mexico, Peru, China, and other areas of the world.

So, despite the beauty and the many resources, the environment of the Southwest proved only narrowly able to support a farming group. In the end, or at least at times, it was better able to support hunting and gathering groups such as the Ute, Navajo, Paiute, and Apache.

CHAPTER TWO

The Cultural Setting

To understand the Anasazi, it is helpful to understand something of both the prehistoric groups that may have existed then as well as the different Indian people who inhabit the Southwest today, especially the modern Pueblo, Hopi, and Zuni. Some familiarity with these modern peoples can help place the Anasazi in proper perspective.

The Southwest today is as culturally diverse as it was 700 years ago. It is composed of three major groups: several markedly different Indian tribes with large land holdings in the region; descendants of the original Spanish conquistadors who arrived from what is now Mexico (then called New Spain) over 400 years ago; and the most recent groups, Anglo and Afro-Americans of European and African origin who arrived in the Southwest from the East Coast in the early 1800s. (In the American Southwest, interestingly, blacks are often grouped with European whites in the "Anglo" group.)

The most important of these ethnic groups in terms of the Anasazi are the Pueblo Indians, the modern descendants of the Anasazi. Several tens of thousands of Pueblos live in some thirty towns or villages in New Mexico and Arizona today. While they speak radically different languages from one village to the next, the Pueblos share a fairly similar culture that continues in many ways the long tradition of the Anasazi.

In addition to the Pueblo people, who collectively include not only the eastern Rio Grande Pueblos but the western Hopi and Zuni as well, the Anasazi Southwest contains three other large Indian groups unrelated to the Anasazi but on whose reservation lands thousands of Anasazi ruins are found.

There has never been a single American Indian, not racially, culturally, or linguistically. To view the American Indian as a single entity is as full of folly as it would be to view all Europeans, Arabs, or Orientals as the same. American Indians at the time of earliest European contact represented the full range of societies found in the world. They included hunters and gatherers such as the Plains and Great Basin people, farmers such as the Pueblo people, and urban dwellers such as those found in Central and South America.

Consider that when Hernando Cortez landed on the coast of Mexico in 1519, the Aztec city that he visited, Tenochtitlan, was then approximately five times the size of London. Consider also that the Aztecs had writing, astronomy, a complicated calendar, intensive farming, and many of the other so-called trappings of civilization including, unfortunately, warfare.

When the Indians were first contacted by Europeans, more than 2,000 different languages were spoken in the New World—almost 250 languages in Canada and the United States alone. This exceeds the number of languages spoken in all of Europe and Asia combined. In the Anasazi Southwest today, at least four basic language families, or "linguistic units," exist. Each has different structures, tonal qualities, verb forms, and so forth. This linguistic and cultural diversity is a major reason why the American Indian has never become a cohesive political entity. It is as hard to get a consensus of Indians as it is to get a consensus at the United Nations.

The four primary groups of American Indians still living in the Anasazi Southwest are the Navajo, Apache, Ute, and the more complex group collectively called the Pueblo. Included within the Pueblo Indians are four distinct linguistic groups: Hopi in northeastern Arizona, Zuni in northwestern New Mexico near Gallup, and the Tanoan and Keresan-speaking people along the Rio Grande between Taos and Albuquerque.

It is also important to remember that, at least in the Southwest, American Indian culture is still intact. For example, every few years in early December I like to visit the village of Zuni in northwestern New Mexico to spend a frosty night with the Shalako dancers, who bless the new homes constructed in the villages each summer. An evening with the elaborately costumed, twelve-foot-tall dancing kachinas and nearly a dozen other near deities, and the hypnotic drums and prayerful chants, makes a Sunday service at the

Methodist church seem a bit bland. Shalako is an event hundreds of years old, one of hundreds of similar ceremonies performed in the Pueblo villages each year, some of which undoubtedly were seen in similar form by the Anasazi themselves.

These ceremonies, almost unknown to the majority of Americans today, are reminders of the integrity of Indian culture still existing in the American Southwest.

Utes

Of the different groups of Four Corners Indians, the Utes are the least likely to be encountered by the modern visitor or make their presence known. The Utes are classified, at least historically, as primarily a hunting and gathering group, and in many ways are closely related to other Plains Indians of the western part of the American Midwest.

Historically, the Utes ranged throughout Colorado and into parts of Wyoming and Utah, perhaps even during the time of the Anasazi. They used the lower mesas and desert areas during winter and most of the southern Rockies during summer. More than any other historic southwestern Indian group, the Utes watched those high mountain lands and territories diminish and shrink as Colorado gold rushes

resulted in treaty after treaty, each of which restricted their historic lands.

Today the descendants of the original Utes are found mainly in southwestern Colorado and northeastern Utah. The two primary groups in the Four Corners are the Southern Ute people, who live south of Durango, Colorado, and the Ute Mountain Utes living south of Cortez, Colorado. Linguistically, the Utes are part of the large Uto-Aztecan language family and speak a so-called Shoshonean language. Interestingly enough, the Hopi, though culturally unrelated to the Ute, also speak a variety of Shoshone language.

Navajos and Apaches

The other two modern Indian groups, not related to the Anasazi, are Navajos and Apaches. While they are today culturally distinct and occupy different land areas, they are clearly related linguistically. Both Navajos and Apaches speak a language called Athabaskan, and most archaeologists and linguists agree that they were probably one group of people when they first arrived in the Southwest.

Most archaeologists feel that, relative to other Indian groups in the Four Corners, their arrival was more recent. Current estimates would have them in the Southwest no earlier than the 1300s and no later than the 1600s, when they were first recorded by the Spaniards. Some suggest that they may have filled the void left in the Four Corners when the Anasazi abandoned the area. Others feel that they may, in fact, have had a hand in driving out the Anasazi. Generally, it is supposed that the Navajos adopted some degree of agriculture, while the Apaches continued a mountain-and-desert hunting and gathering pattern. Ultimately the Apaches achieved major recognition by the American cavalry, historians, and of course Hollywood as a result of their long-term, highly effective guerilla warfare against Anglo-Americans, earlier Spanish, and non-Apache Indian settlers as well. Some time after 1600 the Navajos and Apaches became two distinct groups despite their similar languages.

Apaches and Navajos are the primary residents of northwestern New Mexico and northeastern Arizona today. The most casual visitor to the Four Corners will inevitably come in contact with them. The Navajo people live in an area of hundreds of square miles covering some five counties in northern New Mexico and Arizona, the largest native-owned and managed tract of land or "reservation" in America. The Navajo people currently number in the hundreds of thousands and their population, economy, and political autonomy continue to expand.

The economy of the Navajo involves sheep and cattle grazing by individual or extended families. Occasional agricultural fields are encountered in places like Canyon de Chelly, Monument Valley, Chinle Valley, and other obvious places such as Cornfields and Many Farms. Today more and more Navajos are employed in industries on and off the Navajo Reservation. For the average visitor to the Four Corners, Navajos are most likely to be known and remembered as fine weavers of artistic rugs and excellent artisans in silver, two of several crafts in which they have been involved for at least 200 years.

The Apaches are far less visible to the average southwestern traveler. They have today largely mountainous lands, both in New Mexico and Arizona, and are not especially well known for arts and crafts. The primary group in the Four Corners area is the Jicarilla Apache who live just south of the Colorado border in New Mexico and just east of the Navajo Reservation. Based on the excellent mountain and mesa lands of the Apache, one must assume that the long fight with the cavalry was worth it. They certainly fared better than most American Indian groups to the east.

Pueblo Indians

As previously mentioned, the Pueblo Indians are either direct descendants of the Anasazi or, at least, the group most directly related to the different Anasazi groups. Culturally and linguistically they are complex. It is important to remember that the Anasazi did not mysteriously disappear from the American Four Corners toward the end of the thirteenth century. They relocated and are, to one degree or another, the modern Pueblo. To view the Anasazi as a lost culture as people have done for so many years is roughly comparable to viewing those who left England for the New World as having mysteriously disappeared.

As mentioned previously, the four Pueblo groups are the Hopi, Zuni, Keresan-speaking Pueblos, and Tanoan Pueblos. The Hopi live in almost a dozen separate villages located on three mesas in northeastern Arizona, near the center of the present-day Navajo Reservation. One of these communities, Oraibi, is documented as the oldest continuously occupied town in the United States, dating at least to the 1100s. They live, for the most part, in homes of sandstone and adobe, often multistoried, with several kivas (religious structures) in each village. The Hopi continue to farm corn, squash, and beans as did the Anasazi, and have added other southwestern agricultural crops as well. They also continue the rich ritualistic ceremonials that have roots in earlier Anasazi rituals and ceremonies.

The Hopi are not far from the Anasazi, either in time or in distance. Oraibi is about sixty miles from the Kayenta Anasazi village of Betatakin in Navajo National Monument. Betatakin is near the north end of Black Mesa and Oraibi is at the southern end. In this case, the Kayenta Anasazi migrated the length of a single mesa 700 years ago, and their descendants live there today. In truth, they are not that far away culturally either; and most archaeologists generally agree that the Hopi are, or contain, the direct descendants of the so-called Kayenta branch of the Anasazi.

South of the Hopi villages in northwestern New Mexico is the thriving community of Zuni Pueblo. Also a part of the collective Pueblo people, the Zunis now live in one central village. When they were first contacted by the Spaniards in 1539, there were seven separate villages. One of these, Hawikuh, is recognized as the first native American village to be visited by Europeans after Columbus discovered the New World.

The Zunis also maintain many of the original Pueblo or Anasazi lifeways, including farming, stone and adobe houses, multistoried structures in the old part of Zuni, kivas, and intact so-

cial and religious practices. The Zuni language is unrelated to the Hopi and Rio Grande Pueblos, or for that matter to any other American Indian language. It remains something of an enigma to linguists, but may represent one of the languages of the several branches of the Anasazi, perhaps the Little Colorado group.

The Rio Grande Pueblos today are composed of some sixteen villages or towns, in many respects much as they were when the Spaniards first saw them. They are fairly large communities with substantial lands and fields associated with each town. All are near the Rio Grande except for the villages of Zia and Jemez which are along tributaries. Houses are built of adobe brick and clay mortar or stone and mortar. Roofs are still constructed with large beams called vigas as the primary roof supports. Other construction methods are similar or in some cases identical to those found in Anasazi sites. Most houses in the older parts of the villages share walls, and are often two or three stories high, such that the entire village or pueblo resembles a modern condominium complex.

Most villages have a centralized plaza (or plazas), and all the villages have one or more kivas where ceremonies are performed throughout the year. Most Pueblo Indians, especially older ones, continue to farm with irrigation water from the Rio Grande. They grow corn,

squash, and various crops introduced by the Spanish and later Europeans, such as melons, fruit trees, and peppers.

Perhaps more than any other American Indian group, the Pueblos, including the Hopi and Zuni, have maintained their special social and ceremonial systems, languages, and the trappings of a very old and very conservative culture. They have found their own means of adapting to Anglo culture as they did to the Spanish before. They continue to exist with great dignity, adopting those economic, recreational, educational, and other bits and pieces of Anglo culture that are useful and of interest to them without losing their own identity and sense of place.

The cultural continuity of the Anasazi and Pueblo peoples today seems well established. But the strength of specific relationships begins to blur with the Tanoan- and Keresan-speaking Rio Grande Pueblos. Although there are sixteen Rio Grande Pueblos still in existence, and there were a great many more when the Spaniards first entered New Mexico in the 1540s, they were and are linguistically a tossed salad. Further, there were many villages along the Rio Grande before the Four Corners Anasazi left in the late 1300s. To archaeologists it appears that many of the Four Corners Anasazi groups joined the people and villages in the Rio Grande, changing as they did so and allowing no strict identification of which specific Anasazi group ended where. Yet today, two villages almost side by side, such as Zia and Jemez, speaking vastly different languages, have felt no need to change during the 700 years since the northern Anasazi abandoned their homes.

The Pueblo people are open and welcoming. Once you have visited them, the empty villages and cliff sites of the Anasazi will be easier to visualize with people in them, engaged in their daily activities.

CHAPTER THREE

A History of Anasazi Culture

Basketmaker through Pueblo II

The Anasazi appear as an identifiable group in the Four Corners area approximately 2,500 years ago. Archaeologists differ on the exact date, but certainly they appear within a few hundred years before the birth of Christ. Two developments differentiated them from the broadly based, widespread hunting and gathering cultures—the Archaic people—of the West: the building of semipermanent to permanent living and storage structures, and, more important, the practice of horticulture and domestication of plants. These developments allow archaeologists to identify and track the Anasazi in the Southwest.

Both of these cultural elements serve, almost on a worldwide basis, as markers for the transition from hunting and gathering to a Formative level culture. An agricultural way of life soon brings a host of additional cultural baggage and eventually a more elaborate way of life. Agriculture leads to a variety of other cultural, social, and environmental adaptations that, in time, redefine the group into a more distinctive culture.

The transition from a hunter-gatherer culture to an agricultural one usually occurs gradually. While the early Anasazi seem to have arrived both with corn and a knowledge of its use, they continued to hunt and gather for some time. It certainly persisted as a major part of their lifeway.

Most hunters and gatherers are mobile, with a fairly regular "seasonal round." That is, groups or families move from one location to another on a seasonal and regular basis, often following the same pattern and occupying the same locations year after year.

Historically, the Ute Indians, for example, moved to and around the high country during midsummer, then to lower elevations to harvest Indian rice grass or goosefoot seeds during the late summer or fall, depending on when they ripened. Finally they would go to the pinyon-covered mesas at the foot of the mountains during late fall and much of the winter. In each location, favored food items would be harvested. Should temporary climatic changes affect the favored food sources, many other less desirable but equally available food resources could be exploited. Archaeologists call these stress foods.

A number of misconceptions are commonly held about this way of life. One is that hunter-gatherers are continually on the brink of starvation and destitution. Another is that this "cultural stage," as the archaeologist would call it, lacks a complex and well-developed material culture. Still another is that hunting and gathering people are always confined to the drier and less productive environments and regions of the country.

To the contrary, recent research has shown that hunting and gathering peo-

*A shaft of
sunlight penetrates
the darkness of a cliff
dwelling.*

ple have access to a much greater variety and often quantity of foods than do more "advanced" agricultural people. The environments of the Four Corners and other parts of the Southwest are enormously productive in grasses, plants, animals, and other useable items—so productive that only a small amount of the available and known food items are ordinarily used. Further, hunters and gatherers usually spend much less time getting and preparing food than do farming people. And they spend far less time than urban dwellers do making a living. There is, in fact, some question and considerable quarreling among archaeologists why any group of people would give up hunting and gathering to accept the complications and staid, uninteresting life of the agriculturalist.

The following brief discussion of the Anasazi in the Four Corners region relies on the original Pecos classification used by archaeologists to identify the various Anasazi groups at different times and in different locations. Newer material has been incorporated at various points, but there has been such a vast amount of information about the Anasazi and other prehistoric groups that it is not possible to include it all. Rather than a detailed account of all of the aspects and viewpoints on the Anasazi, it sets the stage for the later sections of the book. More comprehensive treatments can be found in a variety of books and publications, perhaps the best being the most recent book by Linda Cordell, *Prehistory of the Southwest*, listed in the bibliography.

The Pecos classification is widely used by field archaeologists today, and because this is primarily a field-oriented book, it will be most helpful as you visit sites and try to place them in the broad history of the Anasazi.

Further, this section will deal mostly with those artifacts and structures most frequently found on the surface of un-excavated sites—the architecture, ceramics, lithics, and other visible items. The vast amount of materials uncovered by excavation will be less often referred to. Additional information and more detail on these surface artifacts and how to understand them will found in chapters 6 and 7 on interpreting Anasazi sites.

Basketmakers

For the Anasazi, as for many others, once the idea of horticulture had hatched there was no looking back. For the next 450 years, a period referred to by archaeologists as the Basketmaker period, or Basketmaker II in some chronology systems, they maintained a partly horticultural, partly hunting and gathering way of life. Many of their tools and other manufactured items—their material culture—were similar to the kits of hunters and gatherers elsewhere. They included baskets of some variety and color, some so tightly woven they could hold water and be used for cooking; chipped stone tools of obsidian, chert, quartzite and others; nets, bags, and other woven items of human hair and yucca fiber; cradleboards to make babies more portable; and remarkably well-crafted sandals.

While many of these items have also been recovered from Archaic sites throughout the West, it is items associated with growing and processing corn, such as metates, digging sticks, storage rooms, and others that distinguish early Anasazi people from Archaic groups in the West.

In addition to the more portable artifacts from the Basketmaker period, structures of at least two types have been excavated. One is the slab-lined cist, used for storage or burial. These small, shallow structures, built of upright thin slabs of sandstone set in adobe mortar, are found most often in dry caves and alcoves in canyons in northeastern Arizona, southwestern Colorado, and southeastern Utah. Because of the remarkable preservation of perishable artifacts in the dry Southwest, a large inventory of artifacts from this time period has been found. Also, with occasional burials in these cists, a number of almost perfectly preserved "mummies" have been found.

White stripes were painted on this dwelling by its occupants.

Cist at Basketmaker site in southeastern Utah.

The second type of structure was more clearly for living or habitation. This is the forerunner of the elaborate Anasazi architecture that followed in the succeeding centuries. These structures are circular, with a saucer-shaped floor rising at the edges. Although we have yet to find one intact to any degree, they seem to have had a cribbed series of walls made of wooden posts, making the entire structure a roundish hexagon.

Structures of this type have been excavated from as far north as Durango, Colorado, near the base of the San Juan Mountains, to near Pecos Pueblo east of the Rio Grande near Santa Fe. Large numbers of Basketmaker II sites have also been found on Black Mesa in northeastern Arizona, in Grand Gulch in Utah, and other locations. There seem to have been many Basketmaker communities, and the culture quickly became fairly widespread over the Southwest.

What of this is unique to the American Southwest and Anasazi culture and what is more or less universal to all of the world's cultures that have developed or borrowed the idea of agriculture? Clearly agriculture, like writing and speech, is a major event in world history. Without a group realizing what has been set in motion, and in a period of time no individual is likely to be aware of much more than "things seem to be working these days," the culture finds itself radically changed.

In the Southwest, it has been assumed for many years that only the *ideas* of agriculture and corn were introduced and that an extensive period of experimentation took place before the Basketmakers were hooked on agriculture. It now appears, based on work at Black Mesa and in southeastern Utah, that the idea was adopted quickly and applied extensively. This suggests that people who already knew about agriculture came with the idea and the first kernels of corn.

Whatever the facts, the Basketmaker II people soon found themselves well established in the Four Corners and by about A.D. 450 had added enough to the way of life that archaeologists identify a new era for them.

Basketmaker III

Following the Basketmaker II period comes another series of cultural characteristics that accompany the venture of people into an agricultural way of life. The addition of pottery, elaboration and standardization of habitation structures, the adoption of the bow and arrow, and the addition of one new agricultural product, beans, mark the beginnings of the later stage of the Basketmaker period. It is called Basketmaker III.

Since sites of this time period are far more numerous and widespread in the Anasazi Southwest than are those of Basketmaker II, it would seem that the population was expanding. Successful subsistence strategies and social mechanisms of the preceding period probably continued, and the environment may have improved or at least remained conducive to increased agriculture.

The primary change for Basketmaker III was the development and elaboration of subterranean or semisubterranean pit structures for habitation. These pit houses, probably an outgrowth of the earlier storage and shallow pit structures used during Basketmaker II, share many common characteristics. These characteristics are maintained with little change almost throughout the 250 years that comprise the period, generally A.D. 450 or 500 to A.D. 700 or 750. In some parts of the Anasazi Southwest they survive well into the thirteenth century. Basketmaker III pit houses are found throughout the Four Corners and the Southwest. They are often found at slightly lower elevations and over a much more extended region than the earlier Basketmaker II sites and later Pueblo I sites.

During the Basketmaker III period, Anasazi culture began to assume the stability and many of the enduring cultural forms that make it distinctive. Further, subsistence patterns, technology, and architecture did not vary as much from one part of the Southwest to another as in later times. Instead, reasonably similar concepts and values seem to have been shared.

In truth, for the architectural archaeologist this is a rather boring period. Basketmaker III pit houses are very similar throughout the region and the time period. They range in shape from circular to nearly rectangular. They were usually excavated from a few feet to more than five feet deep, almost as deep as the later kivas. Most of the pit structures have a small additional room to the south or southeast of the main structure. A tunnel or narrow passageway connected this smaller room or antechamber to the main room and may have helped to ventilate it.

On the floor of the pit house was a central firepit, pits beneath the floor for storage and other functions, four main post holes to anchor the large roof beams, and usually a low semicircular wall, or wing wall surrounding the tunnel between the antechamber and the main room. Often, in place of the wing wall, a simple vertical stone or masonry wall was constructed between the firepit and the opening to the antechamber.

A high bench excavated into the earthen wall along the perimeter of the pit structure assisted in roof construction. The pit structures were probably entered through a hole in the roof by way of a ladder. In addition to the main pit house, sites of this time period and arrangement often have plaza areas nearby for outdoor work areas. Bell-shaped underground storage cists were found near the pit structure, and occasionally small, irregularly shaped, slab-lined rooms were built near the surface, and were presumably used for storage.

The two critical additions to the overall tool kits of the Anasazi at this time were pottery, as previously mentioned, and the bow and arrow to replace the spear and specialized spear throwers of Basketmaker II and Archaic times. The bow and arrow undoubtedly expanded the capability for hunting at about the same time that crops and other natural plant resources increased. The resulting increase in population formed a base not only for the elaboration of the culture but also for the disastrous complexities of future centuries. But for the moment, the expanded technology and the ability to be more selective in their use of available resources may account, in large measure, for the long-term stability and cultural viability of the Anasazi.

Basketmaker III pit house sites are usually small, with only one family or slightly extended family living there. In several areas, however, the communal villages typical of later Anasazi culture can be seen in pit house villages. In a few rare instances very large pit houses that could serve as community structures for rituals are found. Such a large pit house, almost twenty feet in diameter, was excavated near Bluff, Utah, and has the feel of the great kivas that appeared later.

Climate was relatively uniform, with only minor and localized variations. As the population continued to grow and the culture took on greater technological and social complexity, the so-called minor climatic changes assumed a great deal of importance. They served, perhaps, as one of many agents for change and reorientation of the Anasazi.

Pueblo I

About A.D. 750 or 800, exciting, but architecturally unspectacular, changes occurred. This period, lasting until A.D. 900 or 950, is referred to as the Pueblo I period. It is significant that the term Pueblo is used instead of Basketmaker because it marks the Anasazi entry into village life. Without this period to demonstrate the relative continuity of Anasazi culture in the Four Corners, we would likely assign Basketmaker and later Pueblo sites to entirely different cultures—and would still be wondering whence the Anasazi came.

Although pit houses continued to be used during part and, in some areas, all of the period, above-ground structures make their first substantial appearance. Second, the characteristic Pueblo architecture of shared walls and adjoining rooms begins, as does the appearance of regularly repeated patterning of villages. Many small family units of three to eight or ten rooms occur throughout the Anasazi area, but the first truly large villages with substantial populations also were built during Pueblo I,

A simple pictograph found at a Basket-maker site.

both in southwestern Colorado and in the Chaco region of New Mexico. Especially large, circular, subterranean pit houses used for large gatherings of people for ceremonial and community rituals are also an occasional feature.

Villages were usually arranged in an arc, facing south or southeast to take advantage of solar heat. Contiguous room blocks opened on a central semicircular plaza with a pit house in the middle of the plaza. In the Chaco area, covered ramadas, or open air structures, are frequently found in the plazas.

The predominant architectural materials consisted of a combination of stone, wood, and adobe. The Anasazi love affair with stone and masonry, which continues in the Southwest today, had its beginning in this period. It was still several hundred years, however, before the complexity and beauty of Anasazi masonry would become dominant. Although masonry occurs at these sites, the particular construction technique favored during this developing Pueblo I period is a form called *jacal* [há-kal], or wattle and daub. It is still common in the rural areas of Africa, Japan, throughout Central and South America, and occasionally even in such unlikely places as rural French villages.

Jacal walls are constructed by setting wood posts into the ground at regular intervals and filling the spaces between the posts with adobe mortar. A base of vertical sandstone slabs, simple

masonry walls, or both also provided additional support or sustained the structure if the wood posts began to rot. Many variations existed, and in some Anasazi areas in later time periods jacal became a more elaborate and formal architectural form.

Smaller vertical slab rooms were also commonly constructed for storing surplus crops and other items. In some areas the pit house continued as the primary habitation structure with surface jacal and vertical slabs for storage. In other areas the above-ground structures became the primary living units. Apparently all of these structures were roofed, probably with wood and adobe although few roofs from the time period have survived. As during the Basketmaker III period, most of the structures were on mesa tops and in open areas. But in some locations, such as Canyon de Chelly, Pueblo I structures are found in sandstone alcoves.

Larger formal pit structures, called kivas or "proto" kivas, are associated with some of the larger villages of the period. These circular, below-ground features became an important part of Anasazi life and village architecture from this time on. Kivas, still used in Pueblo villages today, are the center of much village ceremonial and social life. As we shall see later, the kiva's form and interior features symbolize the elaborate ritualistic world view of Pueblo and probably Anasazi people as well.

Kivas were much like the earlier pit houses and retained many of the internal features of the pit house. Kiva walls were occasionally lined with masonry, and it had a central firepit, deflector stone, and ventilation shaft. The large size of even these early kivas bespeaks the emergence of centralized villages and structures for community-wide rituals and perhaps other events. These early structures became highly formalized in later periods.

In some parts of the Four Corners very large kivas with distinctive internal features emerged toward the end of this period. They are often called great kivas. These great kivas seem to have served for more complicated regionwide rituals and ceremonials and became important in the later Chaco Alliance in the Four Corners.

Interestingly, during the Pueblo I period the Anasazi in areas such as Black Mesa and other parts of the Kayenta region and in some parts of southwestern Colorado apparently made a slight return to hunting and gathering. Why they did so is not clear, but it is probably related to climatic changes or a momentary breakdown in the process of village development—a social cause.

At this time many Pueblo I people moved from the lower elevations of previous Basketmaker occupation to higher elevations. This relocation is particularly notable because it reflected a need for a generally good agricultural climate with greater available moisture for

Interior wattle-and-daub wall of a partially dilapidated ruin.

crops. During this period the available zone for agriculture was probably somewhat diminished.

Whatever the reason for expansion, in the Montezuma Valley of southwestern Colorado Pueblo I sites are found in significant numbers along the rim of the Dolores River, the most northern area of Anasazi occupation, along the upper margins of pinyon and juniper forest. In southeastern Utah, Pueblo I sites are more frequent in the higher elevations along Elk Ridge north of the lower San Juan River. In the Mesa Verde, the Pueblo I sites tend to be only slightly higher, as is the case at Canyon de Chelly, where sites are found more frequently on the Defiance Plateau above the canyon itself.

By the end of the Pueblo I period in the Four Corners, village life was an established and enduring part of Anasazi life. This tendency to village life becomes ever more apparent during the succeeding periods of Anasazi culture and is a primary characteristic of Pueblo Indian culture today.

Pueblo II

By A.D. 900 or 950, in most parts of the Southwest, Anasazi societies began a pattern of growth and developing complexity that would eventually allow distinction of several Anasazi branches. Technology, subsistence, and settlement patterns and village size and forms had changed sufficiently to allow for a new classification to be identified, the Pueblo II period. By Pueblo II times, all of the distinctive cultural characteristics that we think of as Anasazi were in place. All the material culture, such as pottery, masonry, and other crafts, are remarkably consistent in form and character and are broadly shared throughout the Anasazi world.

Again the architecture speaks most strongly of the societal, ceremonial, shared ideas, political systems and traditions that would endure, at least in the Four Corners, for another 200 to 400 years. The growth and change during Pueblo II times would eventually culminate in the great cities and population centers that are the centerpieces of the national parks and monuments and which the public most clearly associates with the Anasazi.

Relocation and the periodic construction of new villages, at first fairly small and individualized, occur following the Pueblo I period. The Anasazi began to reoccupy some of the lower-elevation areas they had abandoned earlier. The climate or the continued development of farming and other subsistence technology allowed a reexpansion into areas previously used by Basketmaker Anasazi. The period from A.D. 900 until about A.D. 1130 was a time of summer rainfall and good growing seasons. Occupation of some of the more central areas also continued at this time.

By and large the higher elevations were not used as heavily during the Pueblo II period. Some areas such as those near Durango, Colorado, were completely abandoned and never reoccupied.

The Anasazi seemed to abandon their villages with relative ease and move from one place to another in response to changing climate, outside pressure from others, disagreements within the villages, a splitting off of new clans or lineage groups, a lack of readily available firewood, or some other force. This frequent relocation, at times less than fifty to eighty years apart, is a consistent pattern from the end of Basketmaker III times until the stability of Pueblo villages was realized about 1700 or 1750.

A second pattern during the Pueblo II period is the consistency of pottery technology, designs, and forms, indicating the strength of shared ideas. Despite the large geographic areas of occupation, and the developing geographic differences between Anasazi groups, a great deal of stylistic similarity existed throughout the Anasazi world at this time. Ceramics showed bold and consistent geometric designs almost always in black and white. The use, manufacture, and trade of corrugated pottery is also common in the Four Corners. A pattern of shared villages walls, use of kivas and plaza work areas, and other forms seem to indicate more cultural similarities than differences. Innovation did occur, and there are some differ-

Tower Ruin in the
Needles District of
Canyonlands.

ences, especially to the south and west of the Four Corners; but for the most part, consistency ruled.

It was also during the Pueblo II period that certain political and economic alliances and the regional interaction centers were formed, at Chaco Canyon for example, that had a major influence on the Anasazi. Because of expanding population, complexity of the economic systems, and perhaps other factors, the period may have contained the seeds of eventual disaster for them.

Population increased dramatically in most areas as did the size and total number of villages. Except for a few special locations, the key element of this period is the large number of relatively small villages, each with its own kiva or two, and central work plaza, housing from ten to forty people, who were probably related. The villages, in Colorado and Utah, are composed of from three to generally not more than twenty rooms per site including living, storage, and occasional grinding rooms. Storage rooms and granaries usually outnumbered living rooms in each village.

A major exception to this pattern is in Chaco Canyon in northwestern New Mexico. Around A.D. 900 construction began on what would eventually become large well-planned communities. Penasco Blanco, Pueblo Bonito, and Una Vida were the first three of some thirteen large towns that were built at Chaco. These towns had large central-

ized great kivas and in time apparently too many people for the Chaco area to support. A well-organized, extensive system of trading, based at least in part on turquoise, ultimately led to a system of outlying villages connected with a system of roads. This system formalized the trading relationships throughout most of southwestern Colorado and northwestern New Mexico and appears to have been the base for extensive political and perhaps ritualistic control by the Chaco over much of the Four Corners Anasazi.

Kivas during this time period became elaborate and to a great extent fully standardized. Though variations did occur, the architectural elements of kivas were consistent throughout the time period and within the various areas of the Four Corners in which they are found. The importance of kivas (and the inferred importance of ritual) in Anasazi culture seems to be characteristic of the period. These internal kiva architectural features, as we will see, reflect a culturally well accepted and enduring world and spiritual view of the Anasazi which continues through the next period and, at least in its larger forms, on into modern Pueblo Indian views.

Also important during Pueblo II is the beginning of regional variations among the Four Corners Anasazi. These variations, which become the different branches of the Anasazi—the

Chaco, Kayenta, Northern San Juan, and others—became marked toward the end of the Pueblo II period and during Pueblo III. Still, the overall basic cultural similarity of the Anasazi remains intact.

The characteristics of these different branches are recognized in the ceramics and other artifact remains of the period as well as in the architectural forms. Similarities in the basic technology of the masonry as well as room size, the forms of the villages, and the styles of kivas, and minor differences among artifacts define the different groups. These differences allow us to begin to see at least three separate branches of Anasazi culture in the Four Corners and other branches in other areas throughout the Anasazi Southwest. The different branches may reflect differences in rituals, agricultural technologies, and perhaps languages as well as the differences in architecture and material culture.

In southwestern Colorado and parts of southeastern Utah a distinct branch, the Northern San Juan or Mesa Verde branch, begins to become apparent in the archaeological record. South of the San Juan River in northwestern New Mexico, centered along the Chaco Wash, the Chaco branch emerges. In northeastern Arizona in the Tsegi Canyon system, on Black Mesa, and around Navajo Mountain the Kayenta branch can be discerned.

*Pottery sherds found
near a dwelling site
in southeastern Utah
canyon.*

An unusual, free-standing ruin in Natural Bridges National Monument, Utah.

Other variations also begin to occur along the Rio Grande in north-central New Mexico, along the Little Colorado River, around Zuni, north of the Grand Canyon centering on the Virgin River, and to lesser extent elsewhere. A full description of these Anasazi variants will be discussed in the next chapter.

Important to the general nature of this period, and perhaps underlying the expression of the regional differences, are definite changes in agricultural technology, population growth and distribution, and the emergence of political and economic systems of population control.

In addition to the emergence of major culture centers, a number of recognizable alliances were formed in the Anasazi region. These alliances, which indicate fairly strong control by different centers, periodically arose and waned in various areas. They seemed to be keyed to the spread of new economic ideas and technologies from one region to another. These alliances, variously called the White Mound, Jeddito, Zuni, and others, probably functioned to integrate resources and to prevent agricultural disasters. Once again we can see the effects of the fickle and changing southwestern climate on specific regions.

The exact nature and even existence of these alliances are not well known, and are subject to dispute. But the individual centers of most of these alliances are generally well defined by architectural forms and pottery types. They seem to have been an important force in the Anasazi Southwest through time and certainly during the Pueblo II period with the well-expressed and indisputable Chaco Alliance. Future research in this area should prove interesting.

Other important developments during the Pueblo II period are the beginning of water control, more intensive agriculture, redistribution of food and other goods, and trade in both finished and raw materials. There is even some sense of a service industry developing around the religious exercises that must have been held in the great kivas at Chaco.

The water control projects were built both to divert and to retain water which would otherwise be lost downstream. They probably indicate a need to grow additional food in response to an increasing population, as well as an attempt to control or respond to changes in rainfall amounts and patterns. They also indicate large-scale planning and execution of community projects. Such projects indicate some mechanism for community decision making and methods of implementing community-wide projects. These are important characteristics in the development of more complex societies throughout the world and a recurring characteristic of Formative people everywhere.

During the later stages of Pueblo II, its exact origins still unclear, are the beginnings of the Chaco road system. Roads were constructed from the large central villages in Chaco Canyon to the north, south, and west to connect with other large villages and Anasazi population centers. Concurrent with this road development came the construction of special villages or units within these communities—the so-called Chaco outliers. These outliers contain distinctive Chaco architecture and may have been inhabited by Chaco people. The outliers are found in the northern San Juan, the Chuska, and the Zuni areas. The purposes of these roads and outliers were—we can only guess at this point—for trading, ceremonial, and perhaps political reasons. Clearly they represent a more elaborate system of geographic expansion of Chaco peoples than had been realized, known, or understood even ten years ago.

The basis for all of these cultural developments and the origins for both their form and need rests somewhere in the minds of Pueblo II Anasazi; but the vision of large groups of people moving along these forty- to sixty-mile-long roads to and from Chaco Canyon is indeed an intriguing one.

The final Four Corners expression and the most elaborate forms of Anasazi culture occur in late Pueblo II and in the next period, the Pueblo III. And while they were times of spectac-

A frozen waterpocket at sunset; water was a critical factor in the Anasazi's survival.

ular architecture and crafts, the under-lying roots of final abandonment of the Four Corners by the Anasazi were prob-ably developing during the Pueblo II pe-riod. Their ability to adapt to the changing environment, the increasing population growth, increasing exposure to hunting and gathering groups, the in-creasing need for labor for ritual, trade, construction, and the development of complex systems were all involved.

CHAPTER FOUR

A History of Anasazi Culture

Pueblo II through III

In the Four Corners area, and perhaps other sections of the Anasazi Southwest as well, hundreds of years of cultural and architectural development reached a plateau during the Pueblo III period. Because it evolved slowly, the peak is obvious to us in retrospect; but it was by no means obvious to the Anasazi. For them as with us, each plateau is merely normal. The same is true of a major decline. For the Anasazi the Pueblo III period was both. It is that period of Anasazi culture most familiar to the public today, through the architecture of Mesa Verde and other canyon regions of the Four Corners.

The processes that began during Pueblo II continued to their full development in Pueblo III times— increased population; large, well-planned, elaborate villages and architecture; extremely well-executed ceramics and other crafts; a widespread, well-organized and apparently very formalized system of trading and communication between different Anasazi centers; well-functioning irrigation and water systems; and what must have been a fascinating ritualistic and social system centering on the kivas and great kivas constructed at the end of the Pueblo II and during early Pueblo III periods. Just as obvious, in retrospect, the cultural and environmental flaws that were to lead to the decline and eventual abandonment of the Four Corners must have been in place as well in the early Pueblo II period.

And finally, the regional variants of Anasazi culture, at least as seen through the analytical eyes of the archaeologist, were also fully expressed during the late Pueblo II and Pueblo III period. By this time three major, culturally distinct branches, with relatively well-defined boundaries in the Four Corners had developed, along with three in other parts of the region. The three main variants have been named the Chaco branch, the Northern San Juan or Mesa Verde branch, and the Kayenta branch. These three, each with its own area, seem to express the core of Anasazi cultural development.

It is interesting that these branches did not overlap or merge to any great degree. Their boundaries are almost as sharp as our own state boundaries. The Anasazi must have been fully aware and respectful of these boundaries, though formal trading and communication systems did exist between them.

The other three groups are the Rio Grande Anasazi, who lived along the Rio Grande River and its tributaries in northern New Mexico and along the Puerco drainage west of the Rio Grande; The Virgin River Anasazi located north of the Grand Canyon in Arizona and into southern Utah; and the Little Colorado Anasazi south of the Four Corners and straddling the Arizona–New Mexico border. These three areas are less well known archaeologically and not as accessible to the wandering visitor. Although definable as separate branches of the Anasazi, they lack the distinctive character of the three Four Corners branches. There may well have been other cultural and ritualistic differences also. For example, no kivas have been found in the Virgin River area, indicating a significant difference in religious practices. All of these other groups seem to have left less spectacular physical remains. It is tempting to call them fringe or backwater Anasazi areas, but to do so would be to consider architecture as the only important element of a culture. Certainly one area, The Little Colorado region and its Zuni alliance, was an important center of Anasazi culture.

Chaco Anasazi

The Chaco Anasazi, the most urban group, was centered during Pueblo II and III times along the Chaco drainage in what is today Chaco Culture National Historical Park. Chaco Wash is a fairly shallow open valley with a stream that seldom runs throughout the year, although it drains a large area of northwestern New Mexico. This drainage and much of the surrounding country is probably the driest and lowest of the major Anasazi occupation areas in the Four Corners. The pinyon and juniper forests of Colorado and Utah are not found here except in more isolated locations away from the Chaco drainage itself.

Beginning in the early A.D. 1000s until 1140 or 1150, the Chaco people implemented an elaborate trading and communication system with other Anasazi to the west, north, and south. The primary architectural elements of this extensive system have been found in a series of roads and consistently planned special structures or outliers previously mentioned. Both may have been part of an extensive resource-gathering system to provide additional agricultural food, ceramics, large timbers for construction, meat and other food products, and most likely other resources of which we are not yet aware. The functions of this system seem to have been in concert with ritual and other religious elements, since most of the outliers incorporate Chacoan kivas and occasionally great kivas.

The possibilities and implications of this trading and communication system present many fascinating questions and avenues for additional research. Its existence also expands our traditional view of the Four Corners Anasazi. As nearly as we can tell, nothing of this nature existed among the historic or modern Pueblo people. Although they certainly traded goods and ideas with neighboring Pueblo and non-Pueblo people, they did not have as formalized a system as that of the late Pueblo II and early Pueblo III times in the Four Corners.

The large centralized villages, to date some thirteen of them identified with colorful modern names such as Pueblo Bonito, Chetro Ketl, Kin Kletso, Pueblo Alto, and others, are well-planned, good-sized towns—almost cities. Constructed of sandstone and adobe, the villages consist of masses of contiguous rooms up to four stories in height with large, well-defined plazas. Great kivas are found in each village along with many smaller kivas within the room blocks.

The thirteen large Chaco sites actually can be grouped into very large villages which seemed to be central to the Chaco communities and a series of medium-sized villages important to the Chaco trading and alliance system. The four large villages are Chetro Ketl, Pueblo Bonito, and Peñasco Blanco in Chaco Canyon proper and Aztec Ruins along the Animas River north of Chaco. These towns had between 230 and 700 rooms, covered some 18,000 square meters (or 194,000 square feet) and contained up to thirty-three kivas. These four seemed to be the primary centers of Chaco economy and may have controlled the entire road and outlier system.

Next in this seeming hierarchy of village size are a series of medium-sized villages containing some 8,000 square meters, some ten or fifteen kivas, and from 150 to 300 rooms. Some of these sites may have controlled individual elements of the trading system or parts of other Chaco alliances in the Anasazi Southwest. Finally, a large number of

*Detail of Pueblo
Bonito, Chaco
Culture National His-
torical Park.*

smaller sites, mostly at the ends of the roads and in other locations, constitute many of the outliers. They may have been the primary points for collecting and distributing agricultural and other products.

In addition to the larger town sites at Chaco, many smaller single family or slightly larger sites are also found that were occupied at the same time as the large communities. A number of these are found on the north side of Chaco Wash while the large communities are on the south side. These smaller hamlets may have been part of continuing agricultural production in the canyon and in some part may have provided the labor force for construction at Chaco.

The differences in the size and characteristics of the Chaco villages argue for an elite class of individuals or families who managed, controlled, and may have been the primary beneficiaries of the Chaco system during the late Pueblo II and Pueblo III periods. A few —very few—high status burials, that is burials with large amounts of ceramics, jewelry, and other items, would seem to support this possibility.

One thing is clear in Chaco at this time. There were more villages, rooms, and perhaps people than the agricultural production could support. A lot of Chacoans were living off the produce of others. Based on a number of turquoise "workshops" that have been located at Chaco, it would seem that spe-

cialized craftsmen produced fine and highly coveted crafts that were exchanged for food and other items that Chacoans needed—another step on the road to urbanism.

There also is some evidence for substantial ceremonialism possibly associated with the trading system. Archaeologists have calculated that at least at one Chaco site nearly 125 pottery vessels were consumed by a family each year. This compares with some seventeen vessels per family per year in other Anasazi areas. Such use conjures visions of great feasts with the ritual consumption of food and the destruction of pottery as a part of the ritual. Though difficult to prove, this is certainly within reason and fascinating to contemplate.

Few, if any, of these large towns have isolated room blocks detached from the main unit. Nearly all of the rooms of the villages are contiguous. This is a different pattern from earlier Anasazi building and one which must at least express their close living requirements. The villages tend to be shaped in a semicircle, a "D" shape, or less frequently in a more geometrically rectangular "E" shape. A few are completely circular or round. The introspective sense they impart suggests defensive postures or close cultural bonds of family, lineage, and community.

It is hard at this point for archaeologists to account for such tight villages.

Perhaps they were so compact only to permit maximum use of the surrounding farm lands. They may have become multistoried because of a paucity of habitable land, just as our own cities tended to rise vertically as the need for centralized space within them increased.

Villages at this time were constructed almost entirely of sandstone masonry. The masonry walls are several feet thick along the bases with extremely well-built and designed doorways, ceilings, and other internal features. Many of the interiors of the rooms were plastered, whitewashed, and often decorated with designs in red, black, and other colors. A large number of room features such as wall niches, windows, wood platforms, and firepits were also often a part of the rooms. The fine sandstone masonry exposed on the exterior was usually also plastered and covered.

The construction technique most commonly found at Chaco is called rubble core masonry. The walls were built by first laying parallel sandstone walls and filling in between the two veneers with large amounts of adobe and rough stone. The result, in Chaco Canyon, is some of the finest and most beautiful masonry walls in the New World. It was extremely durable construction that allowed masonry walls up to four stories high to survive fully exposed to the elements for some 800 years following their abandonment.

*Overview of Pueblo
Bonito.*

Interior of Pueblo
Bonito.

The individual rooms in the central Chaco villages are large in comparison to the rest of the Anasazi world. Ceilings were as high as 4.28 meters, and the rooms often contained as much as forty to fifty square meters of floor space. One of the isolated kivas at Chaco Canyon, Casa Rinconada, is sixty-four feet in diameter, making it as large as many modern American churches.

Spectacular as the surviving architecture of the Chaco is, it only reflects many other complexities of Chaco society during Pueblo II and early Pueblo III times. Certainly the research of the mid-1980s has revolutionized our views, not only of the Chaco but of all the Anasazi.

CHACO AGRICULTURE

The Chaco area was not as good an environment for growing corn as was the Anasazi area to the north. Chaco Wash is lower in elevation and has a somewhat lower average rainfall, and the landscape today is bleak in terms of vegetation. As a result, during the earlier periods of development the Chacoans may have been more at risk as farmers than were the Northern San Juan Anasazi. They would have been more profoundly affected by fluctuations in climate. Perhaps as a result of such constraints, the Chacoans developed irrigation systems earlier and in more elaborate forms than other nearby Anasazi. Importantly, I think, they seem to have been less inclined to move in response to environmental change than some other Anasazi groups.

As a result of these factors, and almost certainly others as well, Chacoans had developed, somewhat to the surprise of archaeologists, a complicated and apparently quite effective system of irrigation by late Pueblo II times.

CHACO ROADS AND OUTLIERS

Outliers are sites which have rubble core masonry construction of a rectangular room block, with individual rooms enclosing a Chaco-style kiva in the center such as the ruins at Escalante, portions of the main room block at Lowry Pueblo, and the Great House at Chimney Rock. Although this Chaco outlier phenomenon is well represented among the Chaco and Northern San Juan peoples and occurs among the Rio Grande Anasazi and the Little Colorado groups to the south and west of Chaco, it is not found in the Kayenta area.

The roads run in almost straight lines from various sites in Chaco Canyon to or near the outliers. Some five major roads are known which seemed to service approximately seventy outliers. The roads are forty to sixty miles long and range from about twenty-five to forty feet in width. They seem to have been constructed between A.D. 1075 and 1140. They were located initially from aerial photographs, and in most places appear as shallow, concave depressions a few centimeters deep. On-the-ground field investigations have discovered actual masonry curbs in some sections of the roadways.

Without surveying equipment to lay out these roads, the exactness of the bearings and their almost perfect straightness is astonishing. Slight corrections of bearing are noted along high ridges and at other high locations, indicating that the early Anasazi engineers were probably sighting on some horizon marker.

The reason for these roads is still a matter of considerable debate among archaeologists and will probably remain so for some time. It has been suggested that they facilitated travel and communication between the outliers and the central villages within Chaco Canyon. Certainly this is likely, but does not account for the width of the roads. The width suggests great processions; or, as has been suggested, provided room for carrying long wood beams. In Chaco villages some 200,000 wooden roofing beams have been counted, and all had to come from nearby mountains.

Finally, of even greater interest is that the roads seemingly stop at the edge of the Northern San Juan culture area in southwestern Colorado, even though Chaco outliers have been located in most areas of the Northern San Juan. The reason for the lack of known roads in this case is clear. The research proj-

Detail of masonry.

ect that originally located these roads stopped at the edge of the Chaco area in northern New Mexico, and no one has yet looked for roads in the Northern San Juan, Mesa Verde region. They almost certainly will be there.

Despite, or because of, the complexity of the culture, Chaco cities were the first of the Anasazi areas to be abandoned. Sometime during the early part of the Pueblo III period, the culture at Chaco began to collapse, not quickly, but over a period of years. By A.D. 1180 all of the great Chaco settlements, both within the canyon and along the San Juan River, had ceased to function. The Chaco phenomenon was over. Occupation of the sites continued by Mesa Verde people and perhaps some Chaco as well, but the eventual abandonment was less than a century away.

The Northern San Juan or Mesa Verde Anasazi

The Northern San Juan Anasazi, or Mesa Verde Anasazi as they are sometimes called, developed largely among the dense gray-green pinyon and juniper forests on the broad mesas and in the large valleys of southwestern Colorado and southeastern Utah. They spilled over the New Mexico–Arizona line south as far as Canyon de Chelly in Arizona.

They were originally defined and based on the types of sites found on the Mesa Verde, including the well-known cliff ruins in the canyons. The name has been changed in recent years, however, because most of the people lived in the Montezuma Valley north of the Mesa Verde and on the mesa lands west to Cedar Mesa in Utah. The area corresponds generally to all of those lands bounded by the San Juan, the Colorado, and the Dolores rivers. Except for the tongue stretching south to Canyon de Chelly, the three rivers so nearly mark the boundaries that one can almost visualize an early Anasazi conference defining the territories.

The sandstone caves and canyons which bisect the mesas and sprawling valleys were occupied throughout the various periods, but the major occupation was always on the open, flatter mesas. The major use of and retreat to the canyons and alcoves where the large "cliff villages" are found did not occur until the end of the Pueblo III period, and just before this area was abandoned.

The Northern San Juan branch seems to have been a great bread basket for the Anasazi. It may well be that the Chaco system developed in late Pueblo II times in order to share some of the produce of this and similar areas.

Unlike the Chaco area which experienced a period of relatively rapid growth and rapid decline during its history, the expression of Anasazi culture in the Northern San Juan is a more gradual, measured development. The region is characterized not only by a continually expanding population, but also during Pueblo III by the general coalition of the population into larger and larger villages.

The large expanses of land in the valleys, the red sandy-clay soils on the mesas, and the development of water control systems allowed the production of major amounts of agricultural goods. The Northern San Juan Anasazi participated in the trading systems and developed an extensive and important ritual system centered on the many small kivas in each of the villages. It is reasonably estimated that in southwestern Colorado alone, 30,000 to 40,000 people lived in an area populated today by half that number.

The definition of the Northern San Juan people and their differentiation from the Chaco and Kayenta groups are based on architecture—both its basic technology as well as village forms, room sizes, and distinctive kiva forms. The artistic ceramic forms and designs along with settlement patterns also are different from the Chaco and the Kayenta. These differences are pronounced enough to cause archaeologists to suspect the existence of separate languages among the three groups.

Instead of the rubble core masonry of Chaco, the San Juan people built single- or double-course walls of fairly large sandstone blocks. The blocks were

*The Goosenecks of
the San Juan River
after a winter storm;
the San Juan was the
cradle of Anasazi
culture.*

Structure at Balcony
House, Mesa Verde.

well-shaped into square or rectangular forms and were usually set with regular amounts of adobe mortar between each course. Later walls were extremely well constructed. Individual building stones were formed by pecking the surface and in some cases even grinding the surface almost flat and smooth. Walls are often quite plumb and square. Peculiar to the Northern San Juan was a tendency to build over large boulders and other natural irregularities on the ground or in alcoves, closely following the surface to yield towers and rectangular structures such as those at Hovenweep. They must have taken some pride, joy, and a little whimsy in the construction of the walls and rooms of villages. Towers or tower kivas constructed within villages or on isolated mesa points and boulders are another characteristic of the northern people.

As was the case at Chaco Canyon, villages contain multistoried structures in most of the larger settlements, but individual rooms are generally much smaller. Villages tend less to conform to well-ordered plans and appear to reflect a more haphazard or at least less well-controlled village form.

Kivas in the Northern San Juan area are distinctive. They provide a consistently reliable clue to Northern San Juan folk. With minor variations throughout, they are nearly always below ground, or at least appear to be subterranean. They are usually circular,

with a smaller space or recess to the south or southeast that gives the kiva a keyhole shape. This shape is probably both functional and symbolic, a vestige of the pit house antechamber. A bench was usually constructed inside the kiva. Atop this bench, six masonry columns, called pilasters, were used to support the semi-dome-shaped, cribbed roof. These roofs, which could be constructed with short beams, and which are found so consistently in the Mesa Verde area, suggest their view of "how a kiva should be built." The form quite possibly functioned as a symbol of the mythological or world view of Anasazi society.

Internal kiva features include a central firepit, with a vertical stone or masonry wall deflector just in front of a narrow vertical "vent shaft" that ventilated the kiva and probably also was symbolic. These deflectors also seem to have evolved architecturally from pit house wing walls. In some kivas, a small hole in the floor near the firepit is referred to as a *sipapu*, the symbolic opening to the lower world of Pueblo or Anasazi spiritual and mythological areas.

Mesa Verde ceramics continued to be predominantly black on white decorative forms along with many corrugated and plain gray wares of substantial size and distinctive forms. Bold, well-executed broad bands and geometric design elements are definitive of the period.

Pottery vessels include bowls (usually with elaborate interior designs), large, narrow-necked ollas or water jars, pitchers, and the classic Mesa Verde mugs.

Recent research in the Northern San Juan area has tentatively identified eight large towns that seem to be central to Anasazi settlement of the Pueblo III time period. Each of these eight central communities had a population exceeding a thousand and seems to have been tied culturally, economically, and perhaps ritualistically to a group of nearby smaller communities. The towns all have some form of community water supply and extensive water control devices, usually check dams for increased agricultural efficiency, a series of towers, a great kiva or similar structure of community ritual, and streets or avenues through the town.

Work at one of these towns, the Yellow Jacket site, has provided some absolutely remarkable statistics. The site appears to have some 166 kivas, 1,826 rooms, four distinct plazas, a great kiva, north-south and east-west avenues, an artificial reservoir and dam with a spillway, and twenty towers. An estimated 2,500 to 3,000 people lived there, making it larger than the more spectacular Chaco cities and the largest single village or town in the Four Corners Anasazi world.

Sites like these and others nearby are causing archaeologists to rethink the basic concepts of the Northern San

Hovenweep Castle,
Hovenweep National
Monument, Utah.

Excavated kiva at Butler Wash in southern Utah; note the sipapu hole in the floor.

Juan Anasazi. The Yellow Jacket, Pigg-Lowry, and other sites are presently the center of research in the Northern San Juan area. The older view, based on knowledge developed over nearly a century of research on the Mesa Verde, presented a much simpler picture of the Anasazi. We now know that most of the population of the Northern San Juan Anasazi lived off the Mesa Verde, and that the Mesa Verde was only one of several Anasazi centers in southwestern Colorado.

Toward the end of the 1100s and early 1200s, the Northern San Juan and Kayenta Anasazi made their final, rather spectacular relocation. On the Mesa Verde itself, in canyons to the west such as Grand Gulch, Canyonlands and Glen Canyon in Utah, along the Chinle drainage, in Canyon de Chelly, the Tsegi canyon system in Arizona, and other areas, the Anasazi began to build and live in cliff dwellings. This movement from open mesa lands and large villages to dwellings built in alcoves and caves is one of the world's major architectural events.

The cliff dwellings, whether built for defense, as was probably the case, or in response to more intensive farming of the canyons, or for other yet-unknown reasons, are among the most spectacular in the world. And they are a source of continual interest to modern people.

Kayenta Anasazi

If the Northern San Juan Anasazi area served as the bread basket and Chaco as the great trade center, then the third major Anasazi area in the Four Corners—the Kayenta—can perhaps be characterized as the Anasazi Bohemia. Although during the late Pueblo III period the Kayenta people produced fine ceramics and other crafts, their homes and villages were far less organized and planned.

No great kivas or large, complicated, well-planned communities are found in the Kayenta area. Only in the very latest stages did they move into large, compact communities such as Keet Seel and Betatakin. Before A.D. 1200 most Kayenta communities were relatively small, single or extended family sites with four to eight rooms, some with and some without kivas.

The Kayenta area is located in northeastern Arizona, mostly on the Navajo Indian Reservation, and in southeastern Utah west of Cedar Mesa. Kayenta Anasazi extended over a vast territory to the west and south toward Marsh Pass, within the massive and beautiful Tsegi Canyon system, and most of Black Mesa. They inhabited the bottom of the Grand Canyon to the west, and extended north well into Glen Canyon and even slightly beyond into the Escalante Canyon system. For the most part, however, the Colorado River seems to define the northern boundary for both the Kayenta and some of the Northern San Juan people. Beyond the Colorado, stretching for miles to the west, north, and south were the contemporary Fremont people—non-Anasazi, but similar in many respects, the creators of the amazing rock art in the Canyonlands area and other parts of Utah.

Kayenta architecture is distinct from both the Chaco and the Northern San Juan in terms of construction technology and forms. Its distinctiveness makes it easy to identify. Two basic construction forms are found, one a stone-and-masonry form and the other, more unique to the Kayenta culture, an elaborate wattle-and-daub technique.

The masonry construction is normally characterized by narrow, roughly chipped and flaked stone set in large amounts of mortar, sometimes with as much mortar as stone. The frequent voids in the masonry walls were usually filled by pressing chunks of unworked stone in the wet mortar as chinking. There is very little patterning of the stone work, and the walls are irregular in thickness and size. The walls almost rely on the glueing effect of the mortar to continue to stand. This masonry is far different from the finely finished stone walls of the Mesa Verde folk and the thin, almost mortarless walls of the Chaco.

Rooms in Kayenta structures tend to

Cliff Palace,
Mesa Verde.

Two pots, displayed at Keet Seel, give some idea of the appearance of artifacts when the ruins were originally discovered.

be fairly small, with a large number of storage rooms and granaries in the sites. Wattle-and-daub walls, typically used to form the front wall of living rooms and sometimes the rectangular Kayenta kivas, are carefully constructed and consistent in form. The construction is similar to that described for the Pueblo I period throughout much of the Four Corners, but had become more formalized during Pueblo III times. Upright poles were set into the ground and the spaces between the vertical posts were filled with willow or smaller plant material. These were carefully bound with yucca strips to the upright poles. Finally, mud was applied over the entire wall.

Both round kivas with features somewhat similar to those in the Mesa Verde and Chaco areas and rectangular kivas occur in the Kayenta area. Kivas are smaller and fewer in number, and one has the feeling that they had less importance here than elsewhere in the Anasazi world. It is often difficult to determine whether a room was used for living or as a kiva, whereas that is almost never a problem in the Chaco or Mesa Verde areas. Otherwise Kayenta villages during the Pueblo III period are similar to the others in that the walls were contiguous and villages were tightly compacted and occasionally multistoried.

The most spectacular architectural forms in the Kayenta area are the late (A.D. 1250 or later) cliff dwellings found primarily in the Tsegi Canyon system, in Monument Valley, and to a lesser extent on Black Mesa. These large villages represent a response either to environmental stress or hostility from other people at the end of the occupation of the Kayenta area. These sites, of which Keet Seel and Betatakin are probably the best known, are among the largest in the Four Corners. Keet Seel is only slightly smaller than Cliff Palace at Mesa Verde. There are hundreds of these cliff dwellings in the Tsegi Canyon system alone, and all display a remarkable degree of preservation with numerous original roofs and other features long since missing from sites in the other areas.

In many ways they are also the most remote Anasazi sites and the least frequently visited today. Some sites in the Tsegi have not been visited by Anglos, including archaeologists, since early exploration of the region at the turn of the century. It is here that the School of American Research recently located a number of large, previously unvisited sites. The canyons are so remote that even occupation by Navajos is sparse and infrequent.

The Kayenta display the closest relationship of any Anasazi group to modern Pueblo Indians, particularly to the Hopi who live in villages just south of Tsegi Canyon and Black Mesa. The historical and cultural ties are remarkably strong. For example, the Hopi still use rectangular kivas, make fairly distinct pottery related to Kayenta ceramics, and claim the major Tsegi sites in their own historical accounts.

Kayenta Pueblo III villages are not distinctive in form and do not indicate planning as do those at Chaco. In fact, villages and rooms seem to have been constructed as needed and as space permitted. The rooms are arranged into single family or perhaps extended family units with shared courtyards and occasionally other work areas. The village of Keet Seel is a mass of structures within a large rock shelter. Groups of related people probably drifted into the site from time to time as the village was being constructed, and built where space would allow. The villages lacked elaborate systems for water control, irrigation, or roads as are found in the Chaco and Mesa Verde areas.

Although sites are rather widely spread throughout the area in both the lower, drier valleys as well as in the canyon bottoms, once again the pinyon- and juniper-covered mesas on the Shonto Plateau, Skeleton Mesa, Black Mesa, Kaibito Plateau, and similar locations seemed to provide the best farm lands and areas for village construction, at least during better environmental and social times. Interestingly, although a great deal of trading of Kayenta pottery to other groups seemed to occur, there is less indication of importation

The remains of a wattle-and-daub wall at Keet Seel, Navajo National Monument.

*Betatakin Cliff
Dwelling, Navajo
National Monument.*

Keet Seel, Navajo
National Monument.

of goods to the Kayenta area. There is little sign that the elaborate trading systems developed by the Chaco reached the Kayenta region.

A good way to visit and understand Kayenta peoples is to start with the present, that is the modern Hopi villages, and then work back in time. The important concept is that the Kayenta area as a whole has never really been abandoned, and that the Hopi continue to exhibit a nearly full range of Anasazi cultural traits. At least among the Hopi, the Anasazi are alive and well today.

*A pot lays in situ
in a remote Arizona
canyon.*

II

Exploring Four Corners Archaeology: The National Parks and Beyond

Keet Seel,
Navajo National Monument

Enjoyment and understanding of Anasazi ruins in the Four Corners area can begin only with a visit to the magnificent ruins in our national parks and monuments. Ruins such as those at Mesa Verde National Park and Chaco Culture National Historical Park represent the finest examples of Anasazi architecture and culture. They are a distillation of the tens of thousands of Anasazi sites in the region.

Anasazi sites in greater quantity, detail, and uniqueness exist throughout the Four Corners outside National Park Service areas. For anyone who, after a visit to Mesa Verde or a similar location is bitten by the bug, a vast and fascinating experience awaits him in the canyons and along the mesas of the region. These sites, many of which remain remote even today, provide for study and observation of the past. It is an experience that becomes more meaningful and enjoyable the more frequently it is done. The parks are really only an introduction to a pursuit that can occupy one for much of a lifetime.

Ruins in national parks are often the more urban communities of the Anasazi and also often represent only the latest periods of Anasazi prehistory. Sites of virtually every time period of southwestern prehistory, recent to very old, small to large, can be found in the backcountry lands managed by other agencies like the U.S. Bureau of Land Management (BLM). And getting to the sites can be at least half the fun.

A visit to these sites offers the opportunity to see ruins that are rarely visited, and some that are in almost pristine condition. The ruins are less crowded and can be visited when one has time to examine, explore, and observe the immense detail in surface artifacts and architecture.

This section will provide information that can be applied to all Four Corners sites. It will help the visitor to determine cultural affiliation, approximate date of the site, functions of various rooms and architectural features, and some social aspects and other broad patterns that the ruin may exhibit. It will also assist, as an old archaeologist friend of mine says, in seeing rather than just looking at the natural and cultural world.

The different ways available to visit the canyons and ruins are almost unlimited. You can walk along the outskirts of Durango, Cortez, Farmington, or Dove Creek and within a few minutes find a mass of broken pottery, eroding walls, and stone tools that mark the location of an Anasazi pit house or buried Pueblo I site. You may see, tucked into the alcoves of nearly any canyon, masonry walls of Pueblo III Anasazi storage rooms, villages, or single-family homes. Hundreds of dirt roads leave the few paved highways of the region, leading to isolated pinyon forests, the edges of mesas, and an infinite number of locations of similar southwestern flavor. Camping sites are plentiful and can serve as central points for easy hiking trips or more deliberate and strenuous expeditions into the many roadless canyons and areas beyond. From the ends of these dirt roads, backpacking adventures of days or weeks are possible.

Finally, the ruins are also accessible by river. Sites on the San Juan, the Chinle, the Dolores, the Colorado, and a dozen other rivers combine archaeology with the excitement and gentle beauty of southwestern rivers.

CHAPTER FIVE

Ethics of Backcountry Archaeology

Visiting archaeological sites includes as a given a basic rule —that they not be disturbed or damaged, that no artifacts be collected, and that no excavation or digging occur. Archaeological sites are first and foremost a scientific and historical resource. They are irreplaceable and once disturbed cannot be reconstructed or rebuilt. Like endangered animals and birds, once gone they are completely nonrenewable.

As a result, for years it was generally impossible for the nonprofessional archaeologist or visitor to experience the excitement of excavation and discovery that is so much a part of the practice of archaeology. Today, various opportunities exist for the public to participate actively in research, including legal excavation of sites.

Many other opportunities exist to become involved in the research and excavation of archaeological sites in the Southwest without the destructive practice of pothunting, which is little more than malicious and selfish destruction of these ruins.

For example, in Colorado, Arizona, and New Mexico, state archaeological societies sponsor research projects involving excavations, surveys, and other activities under the direction of trained individuals. These societies have active, strong memberships of professional and business people. They are an excellent way to visit and research archaeological sites.

Whatever form of involvement in the backcountry archaeology of the Four Corners one chooses, it is important to use common sense and outdoor etiquette. Southwestern terrain is rugged, readily allowing one to become lost. It is full of cliffs and sandstone traps that can catch and injure the careless and naive. With a little precaution, preparation, and information, most of these dangers, real and perceived, are easily overcome.

Although the Four Corners has vast areas of public lands to wander freely, there are still many areas of private land. It is important to know the ownership status of lands and obtain permission before entering. Maps showing land ownership are available from local BLM offices. These maps show private, BLM, U.S. Forest Service, state, and other ownership and are also good general maps of the area. These and U.S. Geological Survey topographic maps are good investments for anyone planning to visit Four Corners sites.

We have purposefully not included a great deal of specific information about the location of sites or ruins. There are simply too many, and our philosophy is that those who take the trouble to find sites will also take the necessary care to avoid damage, deliberate or inadvertent, to these precious remains.

The following section will provide information sources and some general areas in which ruins are located.

Inadvertent Damage to Ruins

The most disastrous and catastrophic damage to archaeological sites occurs from pothunting and vandalism. The most persistent and unavoidable damage is from environmental deterioration. But even the best intentioned and most careful visitor can cause a great deal of damage inadvertently. Much of this damage is not immediately apparent and often occurs because visitors do not realize the effect that they may be having on a site.

Damage from visitation slowly accumulates. A rock is dislodged here or a lump of mortar falls when someone accidentally bumps into a wall. Continued foot traffic causes undercutting of a wall, with the eventual loss of the entire wall or structure. It is, in fact, almost impossible to visit a Pueblo III cliff dwelling and not cause a small degree of damage to the site.

The only enduring protection for the ruins is to disallow public entry altogether, an impractical and impossible circumstance, or to provide extensive stabilization to prevent some environmental effects. Even then, the inexorable deterioration will continue until at some time in the future, perhaps centuries from now, the site will be gone. A program of stabilization to prevent damage from human use and from environmental deterioration, with good management of public use, is the only reasonable method to assure that sites will survive.

While damage to sites can never be completely prevented, the effects of visiting ruins can be substantially reduced by an awareness of those actions which damage the site. The type of site, its location, and degree of fragility influence the potential for damage. Open Basketmaker III or Pueblo I sites, that is surface sites, are relatively stable and not subject to immediate damage. They began to disintegrate shortly after the Anasazi abandoned them—roofs fell, walls caved in, and soil washed onto or into the sites. Once completely covered, with only the surface artifacts on the ground to mark their locations, the ruins are relatively stable and secure from further loss.

The most common disturbance to surface sites is the collection of pottery sherds and lithics—either taking them home or moving them from one part of the site to another. Usually the larger and better decorated sherds or fragments of handles or other items of interest are the ones carted off or stacked neatly on some nearby rock. The loss of surface sherds, one of the primary methods of dating surface ruins, determining the cultural affiliation of the people, and studying trade and work areas, seriously affects an archaeologist's ability to understand a site. Examine the sherds in place and leave them on the site approximately where you found them.

If artifacts are left in place and projecting slabs or other remnants of masonry are undisturbed, little damage can occur to surface sites. They remain fascinating and can provide the average visitor with a great deal of information. A little knowledge about the archaeology of the region will make these sites a great deal more interesting. Often those that seem to contain the least material may be the most interesting because they may be older and much rarer. In addition, small isolated architectural features such as check dams, firepits, remains of agricultural terraces, or other rare features are of great interest if you can identify them.

For most surface sites that you are likely to encounter, common sense actions will prevent damage to them. One is to avoid driving on them. Tires will break pot sherds and other surface artifacts, cause erosion channels, and damage walls that may be just below the surface. As you walk about the site, it is also important to avoid creating new trails that may increase erosion.

Another type of site frequently damaged both deliberately and inadvertently are the many rock art panels and individual designs found on cliff walls and near many ruins. There are many ways of damaging rock art panels. They are often "canvases" for modern graffiti and targets for rifles. The worst thing that one can do is to mark on, scratch, or physically alter rock art panels. They are among the most interesting and most fragile of all archaeological features.

Pictographs, rock art made by applying colored clays and pigments in designs and decorations, are the most fragile. They are easily flaked away from the surface of the rock. It is best not to touch either the painted pictographs or incised and pecked petroglyphs at all, and children should be kept from touching them. With enough touching by enough people the rock art will slowly disappear altogether.

In the past it has been a common practice to apply chalk or some other substance on petroglyphs to enhance them for photography. In other cases rock art designs have been recorded by using a technique called rubbing to create an image of the rock art on paper. Both of these or any other technique that involves direct contact with rock art should be avoided. There are two excellent methods for achieving good quality photographs of rock art. Angled late evening or early morning light will bring out most petroglyphs and pictographs about as well as they can be rendered for photos. Another technique, one that is quite fun, is to visit the site at night and use candle light to highlight them. With very complex panels, an immense number of individual motifs and other elements will be visible by candle light. With fast film and a tripod, a variety of interesting photos can be made.

Sites that receive the most damage from well-meaning people (as well as pothunters) are the cliff dwellings. These sites contain masonry walls, a large number of fragile artifacts including perishable items such as corn cobs and fiber, and occasionally even rarer prehistoric material.

Cliff dwellings and other sites with existing masonry walls, floors, and roofs are much more susceptible to both environmental and human damage because they are the sites most likely to attract visitors. Often these sites are perched on a cliff or constructed on steeply sloping cave floors or on older, soft cultural deposits. In some cases, literally only one small stone may be holding the wall or the entire room in place. Other ruins may be more securely placed on ledges or in caves, but individual walls or other architectural features within these sites may also be precarious.

Most damage to these sites comes from climbing into and around them. Walking or sitting on, kicking, or leaning against walls may not immediately cause them to fall but does dislodge small amounts of mortar and loosen top stones. With repeated use, the wall stone and mortar will be lost and the entire wall may fall. With the wall may go a room or series of connected rooms. It is very important, especially in ruins that are hard to get to and have cramped interiors, to avoid contact with walls and other architectural features. The same is true of climbing through doorways, over walls, or over roofs to reach other parts of a ruin. It is best not to climb on walls and simply to avoid going into parts of the ruin that require stepping on walls or other features.

Downslope from most cliff dwellings is an area of prehistoric trash, charcoal, and other debris which archaeologists call the site midden or kitchen midden. Artifacts in these deposits are layered in such a way that they contain a great deal of information about the history of the site. They represent, in broken or worn-out fashion, most of the tools and other objects made and used by the inhabitants. Middens also contain animal bones and plant remains that reveal what foods the residents ate. And finally, burials are often located in these soft deposits. In other words, middens are one of the most important parts of a site. Care should be taken not to walk in these deposits or cause them to be mixed in any way. Continued foot traffic on a midden causes it to migrate slowly downslope and can undermine the walls of the structure above, causing it to fall. Erosion of middens is one of the most severe results of continued visitation at sites. They should be avoided.

Upon entering a site, look carefully and determine which areas are most fragile. Original roofs, for example, may look strong. Never climb on them to see if they will hold your weight. Even if they are strong enough to hold you for a short while, each time you climb on them dirt and adobe are dislodged, and the wood and fiber material that bonds the roof is weakened or broken. It is particularly important to watch and control any children in your group who may not understand the importance of loss of materials or who may harm themselves.

Many cliff dwellings are difficult and occasionally extremely hazardous to get into. They may be hundreds of feet above a valley floor and require technical rock climbing. In case after case, otherwise intelligent and careful people risk life and limb to get into a ruin. Although often the person is more at hazard than the ruin in these adventures, in their determination and haste to reach the site, people will often use walls or protruding roof beams as hand-

holds and risk serious danger to the site as well as to themselves if the wall doesn't hold.

And finally, don't eat lunch or camp overnight in sites. Campfires can introduce carbon and other exotic materials that may interfere with the dating and other scientific analysis at a site. Even smoking in a site can distribute tobacco and other pollens.

When you visit cliff dwellings or other well-preserved ruins and sites, behave as if you were in a museum of rare and fragile items. Walk carefully, don't take or remove anything, watch your children, and finally, be sure that you don't injure yourself.

After years of hiking the canyon country and visiting Anasazi sites and taking great care not to damage them, you have entered a site and find that perfect and rare artifact—a whole pot, a basket, a sandal, a piece of jewelry. Do you remove it and take it to the proper agency or do you leave it? It could easily be stolen or may be about to fall or wash away. It obviously is rare and important. What should you do?

In all cases it is better to leave the artifact in place or conceal it if possible and report your find to the appropriate agency. Mark the location on a map and record as much information as possible about the artifact and its location. You may have done something important for archaeology.

Pothunting and Vandalism

Simply stated, federal law prohibits the damaging, excavating, collecting of artifacts, or other willful acts of destruction to archaeological sites on federal lands. Beginning in 1906 and continuing to the present day, the U.S. Congress has passed more than a dozen laws to protect archaeological resources on public lands. These lands include those administered by the National Park Service, Bureau of Land Management, Forest Service, Fish and Wildlife Service, Indian reservations, military bases, and other federal or quasi-federal lands. It is against the law to collect or excavate ruins on any of these lands, and the laws provide for severe penalties. This must be clearly understood by anyone who plans to visit ruins on these lands. In addition to the federal laws, most states now have regulations to prevent damage to important sites on their lands. Even some cities, such as Durango, Colorado, also have passed such ordinances.

Unfortunately, in this country no law protects archaeological ruins on private lands. As Americans, we value our personal freedom and our rights on private land too much to infringe on them to any degree. The result is a continuing loss of hundreds, perhaps thousands, of prehistoric ruins on private lands where excavation is legal. Legal or not, the result is the same. The ruins are gone and the artifacts broken or sold. In many countries, such as Israel, Mexico, Peru, and most of Europe it is illegal to excavate or sell prehistoric materials from any lands. Perhaps such laws need to be considered for this country as well.

Many informed and intelligent landowners do protect and value ruins on their lands. Often a site on private land is better protected than one on federal land because of the concerns of the private landowner. But in our attempts to protect private land rights, we have given the impression that not only is it legal to excavate and destroy ruins on private lands but also ethical. Through education, we need to introduce the idea that it is the responsibility of landowners to protect and care for ruins on their land rather than to destroy them. An attitude of stewardship of these resources is much needed.

In recent years, the economic value of archaeological sites on private lands has increased significantly. Until 1985, the Internal Revenue Service valued land with archaeological sites the same as surrounding agricultural land. Following a lengthy court battle by an individual who donated a large site in southwestern Colorado to Fort Lewis College, the IRS now agrees that the value of land with archaeological sites is much higher than land used only for agricultural purpose. A number of ma-

jor donations of land with ruins have resulted, and real estate values of such lands have generally increased. These changes have provided a strong economic incentive for private land holders to protect their archaeological ruins as an investment rather than allowing them to be looted and damaged.

Pothunters, whether on public or private lands, represent a group of generally poorly educated mavericks who take whatever they can from any source, with little concern or understanding of the results. They are very much like those who continue to poach game on public or private lands or even worse—closer to those who would trap or shoot eagles, peregrine falcons, or other endangered species for profit or simply to defy society.

Neither are archaeologists free from blame in failing to preserve archaeological sites. Often, as they pursue their research interests, archaeologists show little regard for architectural remains following their excavation. Some archeologists believe that sites can be excavated in any way they choose. The result is often a serious credibility loss for the profession.

Numerous examples of such improper use exist. Probably the worst in recent years has been Salmon Ruins, located on county land in northwestern New Mexico. This major Chaco site with 177 rooms, sixteen kivas, and two

great kivas was excavated in the 1970s and, although not the fault of the excavator in this case, simply left open to deteriorate. Today, although progress has been made, the site continues to erode and many sections of the ruin, including an impressive great kiva, have been lost forever.

Archaeological sites on public lands belong to the public, not the archaeological profession. The public should exercise its collective responsibility to protect sites from whatever source of destruction.

Experience in the National Park Service has shown a remarkable relationship between the kinds of recreation experience sought by people and the care they take with the land and its natural and cultural resources. For example, visitors to Mesa Verde are generally receiving their first introduction to archaeology and the Anasazi. With a great deal of information and uniformed rangers to remind people to stay off walls, watch their children and so forth, those ruins receive little damage, and pothunting is virtually unknown.

In the remote canyons of Canyonlands National Park vandalism is also almost unknown despite the fact that thousands visit these backcountry sites each year and they are not under the scrutiny of a park ranger. Sites in Canyonlands often suffer the effects of inadvertent damage discussed above. Most backpackers in Canyonlands take great care not to damage ruins or natural features in the park.

But at Glen Canyon National Recreation Area damage to sites by the visiting public is serious. In 1982 archaeologists and preservation specialists spent two weeks removing a massive amount of graffiti from the walls of a ruin called Defiance House. They revisited the site less than six months later and found the walls almost completely coated with new names, towns, and other senseless scrawls. Most sites in Glen Canyon suffer a similar fate.

The long-term solution is continued education at the parks, by other agencies, and among the general public. However, if a private citizen encounters someone actively pothunting or excavating a site, or scrawling graffitti on a wall or rock art panel, there are a number of things that can be done that can almost guarantee prosecution.

Law enforcement personnel such as the FBI say that the best thing for a private citizen to do is to collect accurate, detailed information that can be used in court to convict the thieves. The worst thing is to attempt to interrogate or apprehend violators. The best and proper action to take if you witness vandalism or other activities is as follows:

- Take down the license number and description of any vehicles around the site;
- Examine and record anything such as shovels, screens, artifacts or other items that might be evidence in court;
- Observe and record what the individuals are doing, that is, digging, screening, bagging artifacts, and so on. Record exactly where they are digging, and what kind of site it is. Be sure to ascertain that it is a site;
- Observe and record the time of day, date, and other relevant general information;
- Observe and record the number of

people, their ages, and a good description of them.

Write down this information as soon as possible and in as much detail as possible. Notify the BLM, NPS, USFS, FBI, or possibly the county sheriff. The federal agencies will take it from there. If you fail to hear anything about the case in a few months, inquire of the agency.

This information alone is extremely useful and incriminating evidence. In a court it can almost certainly result in the eventual conviction of pothunters and their elimination from the Four Corners.

Finally, the 1976 Archaeological Resources Protection Act allows for a reward of $500 for the individual who provides information leading to the conviction of a pothunter.

CHAPTER SIX

Interpreting Sites

Basketmaker through Pueblo II

While it is not possible to become an archaeologist by reading one chapter in one book, some basic information follows that will enable you to understand much more about the sites that you may have an opportunity to visit. This section will help you identify the cultural groups that built a site, its approximate age, the functions of the various rooms, and how the architectural structures likely were used. Further, with a little close inspection, you can usually determine such things as how many people may have lived at a site, what its relationship to other nearby sites may be, and other information that will help make some sense of a site.

The most striking first impression at an Anasazi site is the different building materials used. Thus, much of this section will involve itself with architecture because not only is it one of the most important "artifacts" left by the Anasazi, but also it is the most apparent, substantial, diverse, and interesting of the many different remains.

There are many valid observations that can be made about Anasazi surface sites that will help identify underground remains—the location of pit houses, buried rooms and room blocks, and possible kiva locations. There are also many valid observations about the location of surface sites and possible associated topographic features. The section will address surface sites with and without visible architecture as well as late Pueblo III cliff dwellings.

Many of the analytical methods and techniques and equipment of modern archaeology both in the lab and in the field have become complicated. But much of the field analysis is fairly routine and within the grasp of many people.

Archaeology must necessarily deal with what actually remains at the site. Only those most durable materials and a few unintended remains, such as pollen grains and fireplace charcoal, are available for examination. Perishable materials such as cloth and food items are often no longer there. Missing also for the most part are the elaborate forms of religion, social systems, languages, and other items that form the full richness of a culture. Only a few most basic and probably most deeply symbolic features, such as kivas and rock art can give even faint, tantalizing outlines of the whole culture.

As you explore ruins and derive some conclusions, it is good to keep these limitations in mind. More important is a recognition of observation or fact as opposed to speculation. If you consider your own observations, however, you will find that several alternative explanations may exist. As you generate your own ideas and explanations, leave your mind open to other possibilities.

It is also important to remember that many of the results of archaeological research over the years are well established. Other findings are less certain but fairly probable. And some, the ones archaeologists spend the most time quarreling about, remain mere possibilities. Some will always remain so, while others will become more firmly established as time goes on.

Basketmaker II Sites

Recognizing Basketmaker II sites in the field is difficult. Because the sites lack visible architecture and pottery, they are much like other so-called "lithic scatters" or sites without pottery and that have only small fragments of chipped stone on the surface. These lithic scatters may be from the earlier Archaic period dating between 2,000 to 5,500 years ago, or they can be of "late prehistoric period" and date within the last several hundred years. Some lithic scatters can be attributed to the Anasazi between these two periods and are known as Basketmaker II sites.

In rock shelters in Tsegi Canyon, Canyon de Chelly, and the Grand Gulch area, Basketmaker II sites characteristically are composed of circular, slab-lined cists or small slab-lined pits. These pits or cists were originally covered with a cribbed roof made of small wood beams and lined with juniper

bark. They were used as storage cists for corn and squash and, on occasion, as burial chambers. The slabs which were set on edge are often protruding through the floor of the rock shelter and are often accompanied by large amounts of shredded juniper bark.

Projectile points on the surface sometimes suggest the existence of a Basketmaker II site. The points, and the association with any nearby Basketmaker III sites, serve as a fairly useful way of at least guessing at the existence of these elusive early Anasazi sites. In sum, you can generally suspect a Basketmaker II site when you are in an area known to have Basketmaker II sites—the major areas are around Durango, Colorado, Black Mesa and the Tsegi Canyon/ Navajo Mountain area in Arizona, and Grand Gulch and other canyons in southern Utah—and projectile point types indicate that the site is not Archaic.

Basketmaker II sites are not known in many Anasazi areas, such as Chaco Canyon, Mesa Verde, most of the Northern San Juan Anasazi (except for Durango), and rarely from the Rio Grande area. That leaves mainly the Kayenta area, with some exceptions, as the major center for Basketmaker II sites. Hence this may be a general origin point for the Anasazi.

It may be that these early sites exist in many other parts of the Anasazi

Southwest but are so deeply buried that no surface trace of them remains.

Basketmaker III Sites

Beginning with the Basketmaker III period, Anasazi sites are more readily identifiable from the surface artifacts—specifically pottery. The sites are widely scattered throughout the Four Corners region, but are always very small. They consist of one to perhaps four or five pit structures that were used for living and storage. These pit house locations which are usually buried are difficult to identify on the surface, but the pottery associated with them is much easier to determine.

As previously indicated, the pit house is the classic house type associated with Basketmaker III sites. Pit houses are found during this time period throughout much of the Colorado Plateau. They continued to be used in some areas throughout the entire history of the Anasazi. It is interesting to note that pit houses were even built and used in this century at the Hopi village of Bakabi on Third Mesa.

Because of their age, few if any of these structures are visible. Most Basketmaker III sites are not in the protective covering of rock shelters or caves, but were constructed in the open, on mesa tops, along the south side of ridges, and in the warmer canyon bottoms. As a result, they are almost completely filled with soil deposits two to three feet deep.

An experienced eye can often locate pit structures by the location of the remaining surface artifacts, the topography around the site, and sometimes by the mere hint of a depression on the surface of the ground.

Even though the pit houses are not discernible, in most cases Basketmaker III sites can be fairly clearly identified on the basis of the remaining artifacts. The site will almost always appear as a surface scatter of chipped stone of several kinds, fragments of grinding stones —manos and metates—and a few, often a very few, fragments of pottery. It is the pottery that will allow you to most clearly identify a Basketmaker III site.

Trough-style mano and metate

Throughout the world archaeologists use ceramics as the primary indicator

of cultural affiliation and approximate age of a site. In the Southwest, ceramics are uniquely suited to this purpose for various reasons. First, the methods used to manufacture and fire the ceramics vary greatly from one part of the Southwest to another. Second, the types and sources of clay (or clays) used to make the pottery vary. These sources often can be identified. Third, the material used to "temper" the clay to prevent it from cracking during firing also varies a great deal from one place to another. Finally, the type of design used and the material used to execute the design change from one time period or place to another.

Most important for dating sites is that these various elements change through time. This process of change, the rate of which varies from group to time period, allows the archaeologist and you to identify roughly the date of the ceramics and the cultural affiliation of the site.

All of this can occur with one more important additional element—independent dating of the ceramics by carbon 14, dendrochronology, archaeomagnetic, or other methods. In the Southwest, ceramics have been intensively and accurately dated by dendrochronology and other means, so that the relative dates of the different types are fairly well known. Such is the case with Basketmaker III ceramics.

Identification of pottery types in the Four Corners can be complex; certain key types, however, can be more easily identified and are the ones that will help you at a site. Many of the others either cannot be identified readily, even by an experienced archaeologist, or are too difficult to be of any help.

To best understand how pottery types change through time, think back about the kinds of dishes that your family used when you were growing up—some china, some ordinary dishware, and perhaps some plastic or metal plates for camping. Think again of the dishes that your grandparents used. In most cases, your parents and grandparents used dishes different from those you use today. Much as our own dishwares change, often in our own time, so too did the Anasazi's, although much more slowly than ours as a rule.

Also, think of those items in your household purchased in some foreign location. These "trade wares" are also important indicators of time and trading relationships. This is true both for us and for the Anasazi. And finally think of those heirlooms, dishes or cook ware from your grandmother or earlier ancestors that your family prizes and keeps. These tend to foul up the whole business and will confuse archaeologists of the future just as they do for archaeologists of the present. Fortunately, these heirlooms are usually few in number and can often be identified as heirlooms. On archaeological sites, unfortunately, these rare and exotic sherds such as trade wares and heirlooms are also the ones most often packed away from a site, so that their existence may never be known.

The early ceramics found at Basketmaker III pit house villages and sites belong to a class of Anasazi ceramics simply called "gray wares." These are undecorated wares that have been smoothed and scraped to give them a rough, even finish on the outside and inside. If you look at these sherds carefully, you can see the scraping and often the smoothing marks on the surface. When fired, they are a gray to light brown or darker color. Varieties of these early gray wares are found from the earliest Basketmaker III sites to the latest Pueblo III cliff sites in the Four Corners. In many cases, in later Pueblo II and Pueblo III times they cannot be identified as to their date of manufacture, but during the Basketmaker III period they can. They lack a slip—a thin wash of very fine clay applied over the vessel after manufacture to hide the grains of sand and rock used as temper. These protruding grains, not covered by a slip, are the primary indicators of Basketmaker III gray wares. The Anasazi did not begin using slips until much later, about A.D. 700.

Ceramics found on Basketmaker III sites are of two general types: Chapin Gray in southwestern Colorado or Lino Gray in northwestern New Mexico and northeastern Arizona. Generally Chapin wares are found at Basketmaker III sites north of the San Juan River while Lino wares are from those south and west of the San Juan. This differentiation, which may have ultimately developed into the Northern San Juan and the Chaco branches of the Four Corners Anasazi, can be determined by the type of temper used in the manufacture of the ceramics. Chapin gray wares have a crushed rock temper and the Lino gray wares have a quartz sand temper. Keep in mind that the different branches or alliances of Four Corners Anasazi had yet to establish themselves, and the Basketmaker culture was generally the same throughout the Four Corners, and indeed most of the Colorado Plateau.

Basketmaker III sites then can be identified as follows:

1. The site will usually only contain gray wares. There will be no corrugated sherds and no decorated sherds.

2. The sherds will be few in number compared to the number of chipped stone artifacts.

3. There will be no visible masonry architecture on the site, including no loose building stone.

4. The sherds are likely to be small and have a very "crude" surface appearance. This crude appearance, relative to other Anasazi ceramics, is the result of the lack of slip.

Although these Chapin Gray and Lino Gray wares are the most common types of ceramics encountered on Basketmaker III sites, on rare occasions, especially on later sites of this period, a small number of other types will be found.

A very few decorated sherds with a thin rough black paint used to form a fairly crude design on the surface will be found. Except for the decoration the surface of these sherds will look the same and have the same general manufacturing technology as other gray wares. On rarer occasions, some of the Basketmaker III gray wares will also be in association with a so-called red on orange and a black on red pottery. These types, most often found in southeastern Utah, are basically a red or orangish fired ware with a simple design in black or red.

Occasionally, a Basketmaker III ware with a temper of basalt instead of quartz sand or crushed rock is found. This temper is relatively easy to identify, even without a hand lens, as a series of small black or greenish black specks of rock in the body of the sherd. These so-called Chuska Gray wares are normally found in the Chuska Valley of northwestern New Mexico or in and around the Chaco area.

To better understand the ceramics that you find at Anasazi sites, a visit to any of the many museums in the Four Corners can be an excellent source for help in identifying ceramics. Basketmaker III pottery as well as ceramics from the later periods are exhibited at the Mesa Verde National Park Museum, the Museum of Northern Arizona, Chaco Canyon, Fort Lewis College, and at the Edge of the Cedars Museum.

The types of chipped stone and the type of stone material vary considerably from one part of the Four Corners to another. In southwestern Colorado, Basketmaker III sites often will have substantial amounts of a red or purplish quartzite; cherts of yellow or red; a nearly white, often transluscent chalcedony; and many small fragments of a brownish petrified wood. In other parts of the Four Corners different types of stone material were used, generally from sources not far from the villages. Obsidian, the shiny, black, glassy material so highly prized for making high-quality points and cutting tools, is found at many Basketmaker III sites, but usually in fairly small quantities.

Slabs of sandstone or a harder, fine-grained quartzite used as grinding stones for processing corn and other food stuffs also occur on Basketmaker III sites. The metates used during this time are "trough" metates.

Arrow points tend to be small and triangular, often with corner or side notches, although a few other stone artifacts such as knives are larger.

BASKETMAKER III CAVE SITES

Although Basketmaker III sites are found primarily on the surface, they do occur occasionaly in dry rock shelters and caves in canyons in the Four Corners. Generally they are difficult to locate because they are often buried beneath later Pueblo III remains in the cave. Basketmaker III sites are found in rock shelters in association with later Pueblo III masonry villages at Mesa Verde National Park and in Canyon de Chelly. Step House on Wetherill Mesa at Mesa Verde is one of the few cave Basketmaker III pit house sites open to visitors.

Pueblo I

The transition from Basketmaker III to Pueblo I was gradual, not sudden, as the archaeological classification scheme might indicate. Many Pueblo I sites contain remnants and many of the same traits that are present on Basketmaker III sites. The primary changes are in architecture, village locations, and the size and forms of the villages. Some Pueblo I villages are quite large, covering several acres. Others are not much larger than earlier sites. But the change is discernible on the surface of the ground and in the artifacts.

Although many changes in the culture define the Pueblo I period, the best indicator of a Pueblo I site in the field is the existence of a new type of pottery. This type is very distinctive, and once you have seen it you will readily recognize it. The use of gray wares continued in Pueblo I, but the Anasazi developed a slightly new decorative form called "neck banding."

Anasazi pottery was constructed by a technique called coiling and scraping. That is, the vessel was formed by building coils of clay on top of one another to form the basic pot; these coils were pinched together to make them bond, then obliterated by smoothing the outside and inside of the vessel with a piece of squash rind or an old sherd until the walls were more or less uniform in thickness. If you examine the surface of Anasazi pottery, you can often still see the original coils where they were not completely obliterated.

Neck-banded sherds are called Moccasin Gray by archaeologists. The characteristic neck bands were formed when the last layers of coils at the neck of certain types of pots were not scraped but only slightly flattened to create a series of "bands." In examining a surface site you need to examine sherds from throughout the site because there are not likely to be very many of these neck-banded sherds. If you find even one, you can determine that at least one occupation of the site was during the Pueblo I period.

Other pot sherds at Pueblo I sites often include a new decorated ware with a black design on a white background (the first introduction of "white wares") and several new types, though usually only a few, of red wares with black designs. These basic types differ from one part of the Four Corners to another and carry different names in each of the areas. (A complete discussion of them would be too technical for an introductory book of this type.) It is important primarily to note that they will occur with the neck-banded types and should not confuse you concerning the identification of a Pueblo I village.

The black on white ceramics, of which the most common are Piedra Black on White in southwest Colorado and southeast Utah and La Plata Black on White south and west of the San Juan River in New Mexico, are of additional interest. Some sherds show the first evidence of a thin, often poorly applied slip. On many the first indication of polishing occurs. These two characteristics become very well developed and very important in later time periods.

Note that on early Pueblo I sites, ce-

ramics will be simpler, much more like those of Basketmaker III sites. On later Pueblo I sites, with neck-banded pot-

Neck-banded jar

tery, there will be a greater abundance of decorated white wares, and in some cases perhaps even a few sherds from Pueblo II. The different types and quantities of types can be used to make a rough assessment of the relative date of the Pueblo I site and what it may be transitional to or from.

A useful endeavor is to make a pot using native clays, plant or mineral paints, coiling methods, and prehistoric firing techniques. The modern replication of prehistoric crafts is called experimental archaeology and is widely used to gain a better understanding of prehistoric technology. After you have

actually attempted to make a pot using known prehistoric methods, your understanding and ability to recognize slips, tempers, paint types, polishing, and other techniques will be much increased. It is also a lot of fun to do.

The surface indications of Pueblo I architecture also differ significantly from Basketmaker III sites and sites of following time periods. As mentioned earlier, Pueblo I sites tend to be larger, and, in the mid and late parts of the period, the sites are located at slightly higher elevations. These high areas represent an actual migration from Basketmaker III regions and were probably in response to changes in rainfall and growing season patterns. The large size reflects the developing social patterns of Anasazi society and may indicate other responses either to environmental factors; stronger, more cohesive social organization; or some form of human pressure on the groups.

Whatever the reason, the sites are distinctive in several ways. They have a tendency to be "arc-shaped" villages, or linear in form. Often a block of four or five to as many as fifteen contiguous rooms form a slight arc around a central, large pit house or "proto kiva" structure. The locations of the subterranean pit houses or kivas can be inferred from the arc arrangement of the room block. In some very large sites, several different components of arcs or linear room blocks are often found.

The surface of a Pueblo I site will have little evidence of masonry stone and usually only a few very rough fragments of building stone. Rarely, unless the site is also part of a Pueblo II village, is there a "rubble mound" or significant mounding distinct from the surrounding land contour. Often, however, vertical stones will be seen protruding from the ground. These stones will define the shape of a roughly rectangular or squarish individual room. This is an important characteristic of Pueblo I sites.

The vertical stones are a characteristic of wattle-and-daub architecture. They supported the upright posts that were the framework for the wattle-and-daub walls.

Many sherds, chipped stone, and fragments of metates, manos, and other pieces of sandstone are usually found on the ground. The sites often have a darker soil color as a result of the deep middens and dumping of charcoal over long periods of time. This is especially true if the site is on a ridge and has been eroding slightly over the years. Although little indication remains on the surface, many Pueblo I sites, especially those in the Chaco area, seemed to have fairly large post-supported brush structures called "ramadas" in the open plaza areas in front of the villages.

Using the surface indications, vertical slabs, neck-banded pot sherds, the fairly large amount of chipped stone

and sherds, and the basic form or shape of the site, its flatness and location, you can generally conclude that a village or small family dwelling dates to Pueblo I.

Remember, however, that the description is typical and somewhat idealized. Many variations occur. Despite the fact that the Anasazi were usually fairly consistent from period to period, there are variations from one part of the Anasazi Four Corners to another and different areas were occupied at slightly different times during Pueblo I or other periods. Also keep in mind that sites can contain both Basketmaker III pit house villages and later Pueblo I structures. And a Pueblo I site can be masked and covered by sites of later periods.

If you have a large site that you suspect is multicomponent or if you are examining a large Pueblo II site and find neck-banded ceramics, even a few of them, you can be almost certain that it had a preceding Pueblo I occupation.

Since Pueblo I villages are usually backfilled following their excavation, there are only a few places where they are exhibited. Two are at Mesa Verde National Park. Badger House on Wetherill Mesa is a Pueblo I site with examples of both Pueblo I and later time periods, and there is a site along the Ruins Road Drive on Chapin Mesa.

The classic Pueblo I backcountry site that initially defined the period is called Alkali Ridge near Blanding,

Utah. This very large site is on BLM land and is a National Historic Landmark. It is open for public visitation. After visiting Mesa Verde, Alkali Ridge is a good second trip.

Several large Pueblo I villages were excavated as part of the Dolores Archaeological Project in southwestern Colorado from 1978 to 1981. Although reports from these excavations are available to the public, the sites are now beneath the newly created McPhee Reservoir.

Many unexcavated Pueblo I sites are found on Elk Ridge in southeast Utah west of Monticello. No publications of these sites are presently available, but you can contact the BLM in Monticello or the Forest Service for additional information about these village locations. In addition, backcountry Pueblo I sites can be found along the ridges along the New Mexico and Colorado state lines.

Pueblo II

The distinction between Pueblo I and Pueblo II sites is striking and the two are not easily mistaken. Further, the architectural and ceramic indicators are relatively easy to determine. It is, however, a little more difficult to determine a Pueblo II site from later surface Pueblo III sites in the Four Corners; but, with a little practice and experience, the distinction will not be as difficult.

Pueblo II sites also contrast sharply from one part of the Four Corners to another and, at least in the Chaco areas of northern New Mexico, the late Pueblo II period is the essential culmination of the Chaco branch. It is in the early Pueblo II period that the large Chaco towns begin to develop.

Ceramics become a great deal more varied and complex, and there is greater variation from one part of the Four Corners to another as different types begin to identify and express the subdivisions of Four Corners Anasazi culture.

Flagstaff Black on White style

There are two key developments—in architecture the consistent use of masonry for the construction of rooms, villages, and kivas, and in ceramics the introduction of corrugated wares and the full development and regular use of decorated black on white wares. In other words, if the site has corrugated sherds it must be either Pueblo II or Pueblo III. If the site is a "rubble

mound," literally a mound of stone and earth resulting from fallen masonry walls, or if there are remains of masonry walls or a great deal of building stone, it is either a Pueblo II or Pueblo III surface site. These two characteristics serve as the rough indicators of sites from these periods throughout the Anasazi area. But the two periods can be separated based on the surface indications and artifacts. Even early and late manifestations of Pueblo II can be identified, as can the culture area the site represents.

The use of pit structures continues during the Pueblo II period, but by now they have become masonry lined and are usually called kivas. At unexcavated sites, these kivas can be recognized only as circular depressions near the rubble mounds. At excavated sites in parks and other locations there are two basic types of kivas—the small Northern San Juan style and the very large Chaco Canyon great kivas.

NORTHERN SAN JUAN OR MESA VERDE AREA SITES

In early Pueblo II times in the general region of the Northern San Juan branch of the Anasazi, there is a definite and interesting shift in the pattern of village location, size, and the technology of their construction. In many cases early Pueblo II sites are smaller than Pueblo I sites, and often consist of four

or five rooms to fifteen to twenty rooms. The sites are usually laid out in a linear, L- or U-shaped village with an elaborate masonry kiva to the south, often enclosed within the L or U of the village wings. This kiva, with its roof, becomes a formal central outdoor plaza with most of the rooms opening onto this plaza.

Not only are the villages generally smaller, but they are also much more widely scattered over the mesas and wide valley bottoms than are Pueblo I sites. The Anasazi also reoccupied some of the lower elevations that tended to be unused during the Pueblo I period. The population seems to have expanded, and sites are generally, though not always, found in the best agricultural areas. At Mesa Verde and in a few other regions, Pueblo II villages are often found on the talus slopes of canyons as well as on the mesas above. Also during the Pueblo II period round and D-shaped towers begin to be developed and become a frequent part of the Northern San Juan culture area. In addition to the villages themselves, extensive water control structures were developed, mainly masonry check dams along the arroyos and the shallow, faint, drainages in the valleys and in the canyons.

With lots of people scattered over the landscape, well-developed agriculture and crafts, good rainfall, an elaborate ceremonial system, and trade with neighboring groups, early Pueblo II and perhaps much of the later Pueblo II period in the Northern San Juan area must have been one of the best for the Anasazi. There is a sense of security about the sites. The Northern San Juan area was at its apex as the bread basket of the Anasazi world. One can almost sense this in the neatly constructed Pueblo II sites.

Experience and attention to detail at the sites will be helpful in identifying and interpreting them. When possible, it is extremely useful to have an experienced person accompany you to some of these more complex sites to help sort out some of the confusing aspects. Dense sagebrush and modern impacts such as farming or roads will make the picture even more complex. But in time and with patience, you will be amazed at how much you can determine about a site from only a surface examination.

Depending on a site's size and location, try to visualize it in its entirety. How high is the site mound above the present ground surface? What is the general shape of the mound? Are there discernible depressions to the south or southeast that might identify a kiva and associated plaza or plazas? Are there heavily charcoaled areas with dense concentrations of sherds and chipped stone to the south or southeast, marking trash dumps or kitchen middens? Does the height of the mound indicate one, two, or more stories in the

original structure? This overall view is helpful in understanding some of the architectural detail at a site and allows a picture of it to form in your mind as you explore.

Detailed observations of the surface architecture of the site are almost limitless, but a few of the more important follow.

The tops of buried walls will often be visible on the surface of the site. Keep in mind that the walls, for the most part, are just below ground or are actually at the surface, depending on whether the site is eroding or whether soil is being deposited. In general, if the site is on a ridge or hill it is probably eroding, and if it is in the bottom of a canyon or valley it is being buried. For example, if you have a site that is actively being buried and can find only a few artifacts on the surface, the site below your feet is probably quite extensive. On the other hand, if the site is being eroded and the artifacts are washing downslope, the artifacts may not indicate where the main part of the site actually is located.

Evidence of walls will be most apparent at the corners of the site, and often along the edges of the mound rather than in the center. Imagine the pattern of a masonry wall viewed from above and you will be able to locate the wall tops. You can then determine the general size and shape of the rooms (at most Pueblo II and Pueblo III sites they

will be rectangular, but notable exceptions and examples of other shapes exist). The number of rooms the site may have, probable location of plazas, and other configurations of the entire village may also be determined. Also watch for indications of circular or semicircular walls that may identify towers or rooms that are not entirely rectangular in shape.

Pueblo II masonry in the Northern San Juan area is generally a single or double stone width set in adobe mortar. The stone, at least in the early part of the period, is usually not worked a great deal. All the rough edges are not pecked or ground off, and the stone is usually irregular in shape. Walls are generally fairly plumb and square, but look considerably cruder than the extremely fine masonry typical of the Pueblo III period.

At this point it is helpful to draw a simple outline sketch map of the site as you think it exists and use the sketch to check your view and to add more detail. When you have finished with such a detailed examination, you will be astonished at how much more you understand about the village— much more than after a quick walk-through in which you mostly see only masses of stone, sherds, and other artifacts, seemingly scattered at random.

Finally, before leaving the subject of architecture, be sure to examine the area around a site to see what sorts of smaller outlying features may exist such as towers, check dams, remote firepits, and surface scatters of artifacts that may indicate an outlying work area or small site of some special function. The larger the site, the more likely that these outlying features will be found. You may also want to examine any exposed sandstone faces near the site or in nearby canyons for rock art.

Three or four types of ceramics, with many subvarieties, are found on surface Pueblo II sites in the Northern San Juan area. On these sites the ceramics become much more complicated than in preceding periods. The four types are the corrugated wares, gray wares similar to those found in Basketmaker III and Pueblo I sites, a number of decorated black on white types, and small amounts of red wares.

The corrugated wares that mark the beginning of the Pueblo II period continue into Pueblo III times, but the rims of the corrugated sherds will define a Pueblo II site for you. Corrugated "body" sherds, that is the base or main body of the vessel, cannot be distinguished between Pueblo II and Pueblo III time periods; only the rims of the vessels are different. Examine the numerous corrugated sherds until you find a rim. These rims occur in three basic varieties: straight-sided, slightly flared, and deeply flared. Each type can be dated. If the rim is straight with a final wide thick band of clay at the top, it is

called Mancos Corrugated and dates between A.D. 900 to 1200. If the rim is only slightly flared, it is called Dolores Corrugated and dates between A.D. 1050 and 1250. Finally, if it is deeply flared, it is called Mesa Verde Corrugated and dates between A.D. 1100 and 1300.

Black on white wares are useful in determining if a site is early Pueblo II or later Pueblo II. The dating of these sherds takes a little more experience and study since they tend to blend through time. Often a single sherd will have characteristics of several types.

In the Northern San Juan areas of southwestern Colorado and southeastern Utah, two types of Pueblo II black on white decorated sherds are commonly encountered. In early Pueblo II a type called Cortez Black on White is found and later a type called Mancos Black on White. Both types incorporate a huge number of different designs and unfortunately share a great number of technical similarities.

The Cortez types were used from approximately A.D. 900 to 1000 or slightly later. The sherds are slipped with a white clay, polished, and tempered with crushed rock. So are Mancos Black on White. The black design is "mineral" paint derived by grinding up a stone mineral, probably with iron and manganese in it, mixing it with a thick syrup of boiled plants, and applying it to the surface of the vessel with small yucca fiber brushes. Unfortunately, the

same process was used to make the decorations on the Mancos Black on White ceramics. Differences are primarily in the type of design and the shapes and forms of the different vessels.

Cortez types have fairly consistent hatching and squiggly lines, thin lines and ticked lines, with triangles and circular motifs. Bowls with thin rims predominate, along with a variety of pitchers and small-mouthed mugs with handles.

Mancos Black on Whites date between A.D. 900 and 1150, or about a century and a half. The decorations incorporate a variety of triangular designs, checkered patterns, and others. The forms of the vessels include large "ollas" or water jars with lug handles and a host of dippers, bowls, and others. Small pitchers are less common. Distinguishing between these two types on the basis of sherds alone is difficult; as you examine a site, several rough observations may help segregate early Pueblo II from later Pueblo II. If the sherds have a lot of triangular designs, they are probably Mancos sherds and the site is a late Pueblo II site. If they have a lot of ticked thin lines or triangles, they are probably Cortez and the site is earlier. Don't be frustrated. Archaeologists themselves have great difficulty with these two types of pottery.

Primarily, these two types differ from the previous dominant gray wares and simple, unslipped, and crudely decorated Chapin Black on Gray types that identify Basketmaker III and Pueblo I sites and from the later very well decorated and highly slipped and polished black on whites that define the Pueblo III period. Where you have these two types you will either have a Pueblo II site, a Pueblo II component, or the site is transitional. As you attempt to place a given site in a time period, remember that these are convenient periods archaeologists use to document change in Anasazi culture through time. Few of the sites you look at will be "pure" or "normal." Certainly the Anasazi never thought of themselves as in the Pueblo II or Pueblo III. In other words, transitional sites will be about as frequently encountered as those that occurred in the middle of the period.

As with Pueblo I sites, red wares found on Pueblo II sites are usually few in number. They are more common in southeastern Utah than in southwestern Colorado, and are usually thinner, with a much finer surface and finely applied decorations.

Gray wares generally cannot be used to date Pueblo II sites.

You may have noted by now that the various types of ceramics overlap one another in time. Not a startling observation perhaps, but the consequences of the overlap are important. By identifying the different types and knowing their general period of manufacture, you can narrow the range of the occupation of the site to within fifty or a hundred years, depending on the length of occupation. This is a process known as "seriation." If you wish to pursue this process, consult *Prehistoric Ceramics of the Mesa Verde Region* by David Breternitz and others.

Other artifacts are found on the surface of Pueblo II sites, primarily chipped stone and ground stone; there are occasional artifacts of bone also. The metates used for grinding are no longer trough shaped but are now a simple slab of sandstone. These slabs were often set in bins and mortared with adobe. Projectile points continue to be fairly small triangular or small side-notched points. Colorful cherts were used for many of the stone tools, but many sites will have large pieces of a black basalt used to make cruder chopping types of tools. The different types of stone tools on later Anasazi sites are not very helpful in identifying the time period of the site. The information they contain about the different functions of tools and craft and food processing is, however, very interesting. For those with more interest in stone tools and lithic technology, several books recommended in the bibliography will be useful.

CHACO AREA SITES

Identifying early Pueblo II sites in the Chaco area of northwestern New Mexico is not particularly different from identifying sites in the Northern San Juan or Mesa Verde area. Like the Pueblo II sites in Mesa Verde, those at Chaco can be distinguished by the existence and type of masonry, the size and form of the sites, development of early pit houses into elaborate ceremonial kivas or other special function rooms, and the introduction of good black on white and corrugated wares.

The later expression of Chaco Pueblo II, however, is much more distinctive and the sites are the most spectacular—at least in terms of architecture and village or town construction—of any Four Corners Anasazi sites. This late period is currently one of intense archaeological interest and research. It has had the greatest impact and change in our view of the Anasazi since the original research in the early part of this century defined them.

The peak of Anasazi architectural development occurred in the Chaco area during the Pueblo II period, not during the Pueblo III as was the case with the Northern San Juan and the Kayenta Anasazi to the west.

Most but not all of the late Pueblo II sites at Chaco are large. Some were inhabited by relatively small family or kin groups. Others were extremely large with upwards of 2,000 people. As noted earlier, there is every indication at Chaco at this time that an elite or special class of people lived in some of these large villages. The architecture of

Chaco sites reflects this hierarchy.

At Chaco the so-called great kivas developed during the Pueblo II period. Though circular as at Mesa Verde, the great kivas at Chaco are much larger and incorporate different interior masonry features. The floor of the kiva has a large central firepit and on either side two long rectangular masonry enclosures. These have been called "foot drums" under the probably mistaken interpretation that the Chaco Anasazi danced on boards covering them. Their function has never been determined. A low bench encircles the entire kiva, and often a group of small rooms was built just outside the main chamber. Many Chaco great kivas also have a recessed area to the south that gives them something of a keyhole shape. When roofed, such as in the restoration of the great kiva at Aztec, they are impressive structures that could have accommodated scores of people.

The surface of the ground at unexcavated Chaco sites is a mass of pot sherds and fragments of stone chips. By one estimate, there are far more individual pots represented at these sites than ordinary use can explain. They suggest that many pots, especially corrugated ones, were broken ceremonially.

Ceramics at Chaco Pueblo II sites are generally similar to the ceramics at Mesa Verde during this time period. Both corrugated and black on white decorated sherds are common. The decorated wares have a different temper, and the designs on the pots are different from the Mesa Verde types.

Early Pueblo II Chaco-style sites are more diverse in form than the later large town sites, but are generally linear and usually about two rooms deep. A pit structure or kiva is usually found west of the linear room block. Small late Pueblo II sites, contemporaneous with the large towns for the most part, have no distinct form and vary even more. Most are irregular rectangles with individual rooms extending from the main block of contiguous rooms in various places.

In addition to the large size of late Pueblo II sites at Chaco, a major difference between early and late Pueblo II is the location of kivas. By later Pueblo II times kivas are usually within the room block and surrounded by walls on all four sides. A second major difference is the first use of a masonry construction technique characteristic of the Chaco people called rubble core or cored wall construction.

The early Pueblo II sites use either "simple" or "compound" wall construction very similar to that in the Northern San Juan area. A simple wall is constructed of single stones usually with little or no chipping or flaking. Compound walls are two stones of varying thicknesses set side by side or overlapping to form a slightly thicker wall. These types of masonry can often be recognized at the surface and will help in roughly determining the relative date of the site.

Rubble core walls are distinctive and very characteristic of Chaco style sites. The walls are usually quite thick and are constructed by laying two "veneers" of fairly small, well-selected, and well-shaped and worked stone on either side of a filling of stone and mortar. This type of masonry was probably used at Chaco to provide support for the massive walls, three and four stories high, and the large rooms found in the large town sites. This type of construction is common at Chaco Canyon and identifies Chacoan influence in the Northern San Juan, Canyon de Chelly, and other parts of the Anasazi world. It seems to have been used rarely by the Northern San Juan and Kayenta people, but occasionally occurs in Kayenta sites at Wupatki near Flagstaff, Arizona.

Chaco towns of the late Pueblo II period are so large and so distinctive that they are almost impossible not to recognize. Most of these towns are found in Chaco Canyon within Chaco Culture National Historical park. Additional town sites are found to the north at Aztec, Salmon, and a number of other sites along the San Juan and to the south of the Chaco park. A number of the larger sites in southwestern Colorado, such as Lowry and Escalante ruins, have Chaco-style walls. The so-called Chaco outliers, which also belong to this late Pueblo II period, have the same type of masonry and enclosed kivas as at Chaco in both the large towns and the smaller villages.

Great kivas are usually easy to locate on the surface because they almost always appear as a large, round, distinct depression in the ground. If you find a site that you suspect is Chaco based on the masonry, its location, shape or size, and the ceramics, it is worthwhile to search around the main site area to see if a great kiva depression can be found.

As indicated earlier, the general character of Chaco ceramics is similar to that of the Northern San Juan. There are differences, however, that identify them as perhaps being produced and used in the Chaco area. These differences are in the temper, design, and many of the shapes. Corrugated wares also contain a temper that defines them as either Chaco or used by the Chaco and manufactured in the Chuska Mountain area.

The primary types of decorated ceramics found on Chaco sites are called Red Mesa Black on White and Kiatuthlanna Black on White in the early Pueblo II period. Escavada, Puerco, and Chaco black on whites are characteristic later in the period.

It is not especially important to be able to identify all the specific types, but if you have sherds with a crushed sandstone temper, long-necked mugs, and the peculiar narrow hatching typi-

cal and distinctive of the Chaco wares, in combination with the other charac-

Chaco Black on White

teristics listed above for architecture and location, you probably have found a Chaco site.

KAYENTA SITES

Pueblo II Kayenta sites are not as spectacular as the Chaco nor as extensive as Northern San Juan or Mesa Verde sites. Throughout the period, sites remain scattered and appear to represent small family groups or at best extended families. There are no large Pueblo II villages in the Kayenta region.

However, the same ceramic and architectural indicators used to mark the beginning of Pueblo II in the other areas also apply in the Kayenta. These in-

clude increased use of black on white ceramics, the introduction and use of corrugated utility wares, the more frequent use of masonry for room construction, and the formalization and constant association of the subterranean kiva or ceremonial pit structure with the sites. Some Pueblo II sites in the Kayenta region do not have kivas, but seem to have relied on kivas at other villages for ceremonial or community gatherings.

Sites are small, linear in form, and scattered throughout Shonto Plateau, Black Mesa, Navajo Mountain, Glen Canyon, and other parts of northeastern Arizona and southeastern Utah.

In northeastern Arizona near Flagstaff, at Wupatki National Monument, an interesting set of Kayenta sites from the late Pueblo II and early Pueblo III periods are found. They were constructed not only of sandstone, but also limestone and basalt. They seem consistently, during the Pueblo II period, to be small four- and five-room structures perched at the edges of mesas and cliffs with enclosed plazas. Many of these sites, confined mostly to the backcountry parts of the monument, seem to have kivas or similar subterranean rooms just east of the main room block. They are interesting family units or farmsteads in nice locations and all have a good view of the surrounding mesas, canyons, and mountains near Flagstaff.

The Wupatki sites seem to represent the Kayenta people, but a red and black pottery is also found there that archaeologists associate with another group of people known as the Sinagua; they were probably a variant of the Kayenta Anasazi or an Anasazi group making a different kind of ceramics. It is certainly worth a visit to the backcountry sites in Wupatki to view some of these ruins. The site of "Crack in Rock" and nearby mesas can be visited with Park Service permission. Not only are they in spectacular locations, but they also include hundreds of interesting rock art panels.

The ceramics found on the surface of Pueblo II sites in the Kayenta region are again similar to those from the Mesa Verde and Chaco regions. Corrugated and black on white decorated pot sherds are common. The temper most often used in Kayenta ceramics, called Tusayan Wares, is a fine sand almost impossible to see even with a hand lens. The decorations are different from the other two areas as well. Types are known as Sosi, Flagstaff, Dogozibito, Black Mesa, and others.

Black Mesa Black on White

By the end of the Pueblo II period in the Kayenta region, these more western Anasazi also began to congregate into larger and larger villages. They never constructed towns of the size and complexity of the Chaco and never seem to have had the concentration of population that existed at Mesa Verde. But the final expression of them during the Pueblo III period has left us with some of the finest examples of Anasazi ceramics and a number of spectacular villages tucked into the large sandstone caves in the Tsegi region.

The Pueblo II period seems to have been one of general ease for them as well as the Northern San Juan peoples; and like them, they probably had little idea what problems the next century would bring.

CHAPTER SEVEN

Interpreting Sites

Pueblo II through III

During the Pueblo III period in the Four Corners, generally between A.D. 1150 and 1300, all the previous developments—elaboration in ceramics, architectural achievements, social, economic, and ritual development —peaked for the Anasazi. At least a casual examination of the ruins would seem to indicate that this was the case. In fact, we now know that because the Chaco phenomenon had largely disappeared by Pueblo III, leaving only the Northern San Juan and Kayenta people as definable Four Corners groups, the basic forces that caused the Four Corners to be emptied of the Anasazi had already begun to affect their society.

By about 1170 most Chaco sites were abandoned by Chaco peoples. Ordinarily Chaco sites were no longer occupied by them after that time. Northern San Juan groups from southwestern Colorado filtered south and reoccupied many of the Chaco sites, introducing their particular styles of masonry and ceramics. The Mesa Verde people often used the same town sites that the Chaco had built, altering them to make the rooms smaller. They also constructed numerous Mesa Verde–style kivas within the room blocks at the large sites. Aztec Pueblo, Salmon Ruins, and several of the large sites at Chaco show the effect of this reoccupation. The surface indications of this reuse of a site by San Juan peoples at an unexcavated late Pueblo II Chaco town site would nor-

mally have Mesa Verde ceramics, or if some architecture is visible you might find typical double-stone, pecked-surface Mesa Verde stone.

In the Northern San Juan area, several events during Pueblo III time will help you identify sites of the period. Most of the small Pueblo II villages or family farmsteads were abandoned or expanded, and people began to form larger aggregated communities. As a result, there are fewer Pueblo III villages in general, but most of them are much larger than any built in the Northern San Juan area before.

Most Pueblo III surface sites in southwestern Colorado—on the Mesa Verde itself and in the Montezuma Valley below—are large, high mounds of rock and soil with large surface depressions that mark the location of kivas. Most of these villages or towns have deep multileveled rooms in parts of the ruins. Some examples of these large surface villages are the Far View Group, Pipe Shrine House, and others in Mesa Verde National Park. In Montezuma Valley, the Sand Canyon Pueblo, Goodman Point Ruin, Yucca House, Yellow Jacket and Lowry ruins, and hundreds of smaller villages are found in the bean fields and on wooded BLM lands.

To assure that you are seeing a Pueblo III site regardless of size, examine the building stone. Or if you can find one, observe the top of a wall in the mound and note the type of construction of the wall and the way the stones are worked.

Classic Pueblo III Northern San Juan or Mesa Verde masonry is built of the most carefully worked sandstone. The sandstone in the area is fairly hard and lends itself to the painstaking pecking necessary to render the surface nearly flat and the stone nearly perfectly square or rectangular. These "dimpled" sandstone blocks will always define a Pueblo III site. Set a couple of these perfectly made stones side by side and add a small amount of good adobe mortar and you have a classic Mesa Verde wall. Nearly plumb and with nearly perfectly square corners, the walls are evenly thick and evidence excellent construction.

Second, ceramics of the Pueblo III in the Mesa Verde are also excellent and are clearly the culmination of hundreds of centuries of work in the ceramic industry by the Anasazi.

Several types are predominant. Throughout the Northern San Juan area, the black on white decorated sherds have broad, bold, geometric designs. Bowls usually have flat, "ticked" rims—that is, the rims have dots of paint on them. These types are called Mesa Verde Black on White and McElmo Black on White and are very distinctive of the culture area and the time period.

If you can find a corrugated rim sherd, it will be widely and deeply flared. Large corrugated jars, probably for holding water, are called Mesa Verde Corrugated Wares and were made between 1250 and 1300. They are the latest and finest types of corrugated ceramics found in the Anasazi region. After the Anasazi (or what was left of them) moved south, corrugated wares were no longer manufactured.

Mesa Verde
Black on White

In the Kayenta region two types of the many ceramics made will date a site to the Pueblo III period. Kayenta Black on White, with a later relative, Betatakin Black on White, are probably the most artistic ceramics ever made in the Four Corners. These vessels have an almost pure white background with finely applied black paint covering so much of the surface that the design actually appears as a white on black.

In addition to the fine black and white wares, the Kayenta peoples began, or more properly continued, the production and elaboration of polychrome pots. These are pots with more than two colors used in the decoration. Polychrome sherds will have red or orange backgrounds with white, black, and red designs on them.

Although early Pueblo III sites in the Kayenta area cannot match the large villages of the Northern San Juan people or the great towns of the Chaco, the crafts are perhaps the best in the Anasazi world. The population remained small in the Kayenta region but spread widely from Flagstaff to the Grand Canyon and from Monument Valley to the Lake Powell area.

During the early part of the Pueblo III period, from 1150 to about 1200 or so, most Pueblo III sites were in the open on mesa tops, as continuations of previous Pueblo II villages. But toward the late 1100s and continuing into the mid 1200s, Anasazi by the hundreds left the open areas and canyon bottoms and constructed villages in the larger rock alcoves, building such well known sites as Keet Seel, Betatakin, and Bat Woman House.

In the Kayenta area, as at Mesa Verde, Grand Gulch, Canyonlands, Canyon de Chelly, and in other locations, the best known and most spectacular era of Anasazi architecture took place with the construction of the cliff dwellings. These remains are ubiquitous in the Four Corners region and within the dozen or so parks and monuments in the area. It is important to remember, however, that the cliff dwelling era is a relatively short part of Anasazi prehistory and not particularly typical. It probably reflects the Northern San Juan and Kayenta peoples, and to some extent people throughout the Colorado Plateau, in a state of intense stress. The stress eventually caused a series of major relocations for the Anasazi in the Southwest resulting in the desertion of the Four Corners region by all of the Anasazi except the Hopi descendants of the Kayenta peoples.

Late Anasazi Cliff Sites

The large cliff dwellings built in the final stages of the Anasazi occupation of the Four Corners are certainly the most interesting of all Anasazi sites. Because they are so highly visible, they are the sites that you are most likely to visit as you hike the canyons of the area. Because they were constructed in sandstone alcoves, they generally are not covered with earth or as subject to erosion as earlier sites on the mesas above. Many of the walls and rooms of the villages are still standing, much as they were when they were abandoned in the late 1200s.

The standing walls, original ceilings, plaster, and other architectural details in cliff sites allow close examination of Anasazi architecture. Here it is possible to see the stonework and wall construction techniques that help identify the different Anasazi culture groups. In these sites small fragments of perishable artifacts like baskets, sandals, and cordage as well as pottery and stone can also be found. And in their location, the plans of the villages, and other aspects these sites demonstrate some of the social and religious frameworks of the Anasazi.

Because the Chaco people had abandoned their great villages and had moved or blended with other Anasazi by the time the cliff dwellings were constructed, it is primarily in the Mesa Verde and Kayenta areas that the cliff sites are located. As you visit them, keep in mind also that almost thirteen centuries of Anasazi existence in the Four Corners was about to come to an end. The cliff villages and towns are the last expression of the Anasazi before they left to eventually become known as the Pueblo Indians.

CLASSIC MESA VERDE— NORTHERN SAN JUAN STYLE SITES

As previously mentioned, so-called classic Mesa Verde or Northern San Juan Anasazi walls were constructed of rectangular or, in some cases, nearly square sandstone blocks. It is in the late walls of the cliff dwellings that the masonry can be most closely examined. Each stone has been carefully worked. All of the rough edges have been chipped off, usually with a large stone maul, and then the surface of the stone has been carefully and lightly pecked to remove minor rough edges and make the stone even across its surface. In some cases the rock has even been ground to make it almost perfectly smooth before placing it in the wall in a bed of wet adobe mortar. The stones are about the same size and, at places like Mesa Verde and at Hovenweep, walls are built with almost square corners and are vertically plumb. They also fashioned curved and circular walls and often shaped the stone to fit the arc of the curve.

The stones, again in their "classic" form, are usually set side by side, two wide, and evenly spaced. The walls have no inner core of mortar and stone such as those found at Chaco Canyon. The masonry walls of the Mesa Verde cliff ruins are among the finest left by prehistoric American Indians. They are truly impressive to view. In some cases, mostly at Mesa Verde itself and other nearby parks and monuments, the buildings are up to four stories high and have circular towerlike structures as well as rectangular forms. Outside the parks, in the backcountry, sites will more often be single story or at best two stories, but of similar construction.

One of the most characteristic details of Anasazi masonry, among the Mesa Verde people especially, is the use of chinking between the courses of masonry. Chinking stones were small flat stones pressed into the mortar while it was still wet, to force the mortar more firmly into place and further stabilize the walls. The result is a pattern of small stones in each course that adds further interest to the walls.

Unfortunately these classic walls are not always the most commonly found type of construction. The Anasazi varied their construction as much as we do. In many cases, during the later periods, the stone was not as carefully worked. Walls often are made of irregular sandstone blocks of different sizes, and often the stone is not worked at all. In most cliff sites you will find, however, that the use of double stones will mark a Northern San Juan or Mesa Verde, as opposed to, for example, a Kayenta wall.

This construction form combined with Mesa Verde or McElmo Black on White ceramics and inverted lipped, large, corrugated jars will allow you to assume safely that it is a Northern San Juan or Mesa Verde area site.

If you are in southwestern Colorado or southeastern Utah on or east of Cedar Mesa, the sites will nearly always be Mesa Verde–style sites. It is in the border area west of Comb Ridge and south of Glen Canyon that occasional Kayenta sites will also be found nearby or mixed with Northern San Juan sites. Mesa Verde construction styles will also be found as far south as Canyon de Chelly. It will also be the later style of construction in many of the great

Chaco towns in northwestern New Mexico.

The cliff ruins themselves consist of rooms and other features of various sizes and forms. Compared to our own rooms or those of the Chaco people, they are almost always fairly small. They vary from one- or two-room granaries tucked into small, narrow, low alcoves to 200-room villages set in cavernous rock shelters. Fitting these villages into the available size and form of the alcove resulted in a bewildering maze of rooms and passages with structures clinging to steep slopes, structures built to conform to large boulders laying in the floor of the cave, and kivas crammed in wherever there was space. These villages have no neat, well-planned E, D, or circular shapes evident on the surface sites. Further, based on the detailed tree-ring studies that date these sites, the villages grew haphazardly as small groups of people moved into the alcoves at different times. The final result, though a visual delight, presents a view of architectural confusion and frustration.

Room Function

As you carefully examine a site, there is a great deal that you can determine about it and its builders from the architecture alone—such things as room function, family units, and probable number of people who lived at the site. For example, certain readily apparent

combinations of characteristics can be used to determine the function of each of the rooms. In some cases, you can identify individual clusters of rooms used by individual families.

There are four or five different kinds of rooms in most sites. These are living or habitation rooms, general storage rooms, specialized food storage structures usually called granaries, kivas and other ritualistic rooms, and within or near the rooms themselves plazas, work areas, and passageways or streets through the village. In some of the larger sites, a few specialized rooms were set aside for grinding corn and other food processing.

Granaries are among the easiest to locate. Examine a room carefully and if it has many of the following characteristics you can safely assume that it is a granary.

Granaries are usually smaller than other structures, but not always; some are very large. They will be well-finished on the outside, often plastered, with many chinking stones. The mortar will be carefully fitted against the floor and ceiling of the cave to seal the room tightly. They are usually in the back or to the sides of other structures. The inside of the room is unfinished, that is there will be rough stone protruding from the walls, and rarely will the interior be plastered. The floor, if it is on bedrock, will not be leveled but will conform to the original sandstone floor of the cave; and there will be no smoke blackening on the inside.

Look carefully at the door of the room. You will have noticed by now that the doors to the rooms vary in size and shape. Granaries nearly always have small rectangular doors, and there will often be a groove along the sides and at the base of the door so that a stone could be tightly fitted and sealed with adobe mortar. Finally, look closely at the wall on either side of the door for traces of fiber loops set in the mortar. These were placed so a stick could be inserted in front of the door to secure it.

Living rooms have almost the opposite set of characteristics. They are usually slightly larger than other rooms, but again not always. Very small rooms were sometimes used for living, cooking, and other household tasks. If there is a firepit in the floor, you almost certainly have a living room. In addition, the floor will be flattened and covered with adobe or stone. Interior walls are often plastered, and usually the room will have some smoke blackening on the walls. The doors are either T-shaped or rectangular and larger than those of the granaries and other structures. If the roof is intact and has a square opening in it, or if there is no obvious doorway, entrance to the room was by ladder through the roof. Many rooms with a roof entryway were living rooms, but granaries and storage rooms also had

roof-top entry. Living rooms are often toward the front of the ruin or on the second story. Unfortunately because of their location they are often the first rooms lost to erosion; as a result, many of the rooms that exist as piles of stone rubble at the base of the cliff may have been living rooms originally.

General storage rooms are much more difficult to identify and are always a question. If the room is finished on the inside, but with no floor features or interior smoke blackening, it may well be a general storage room. Some "apartments" or family room clusters do not have storage rooms. Certain specialized storage rooms, such as those closely associated with kivas, may have served as "clan rooms" where religious objects and dance costumes were stored. Canyon de Chelly seems to have a number of these, and many rooms found near the great kivas may have functioned in this manner.

In the Mesa Verde area, kivas are the easiest rooms to identify with certainty. They are circular, below-ground rooms, lined with excellent masonry. The best masons in the villages and the most care in the construction seems to be common with kivas. If the site has been excavated, such as many of the ruins at Mesa Verde, and you can see the floor features, Mesa Verde–style kivas will display a number of remarkable interior features. These special features, many of which are architectural sym-

bols of Anasazi and Pueblo religious and world view, are remarkably consistent in form and occur in kiva after kiva. They are one of the most distinctive aspects of Anasazi architecture.

Northern San Juan or Mesa Verde–style kivas will often have a low bench inside circling the outside wall of the kiva. On this bench will rest usually six masonry columns spaced more or less equally apart. These columns, or pilasters, were used to support the interesting roof which in many Four Corners cliff dwelling sites is still intact or partially so. In some cases the entire kiva is in nearly perfect condition, just as it was when the Anasazi left. As a result we know a great deal about the architecture of these Northern San Juan kivas.

The floor will have a central firepit in a number of construction forms— sometimes lined with adobe, sometimes with stone, and sometimes with a stone in the base of the pit.

In the southern or southeastern part of the kiva the wall is expanded or, as it is more often referred to, recessed at bench level. This gives the kiva an overall "keyhole" shape when viewed from above. A small opening in the kiva wall below the recess extends under it then rises vertically behind it to emerge as a small hole in the surface of the ground. This passage is a ventilation shaft to provide fresh air into an otherwise hopelessly smoky room. And finally there will be a low stone wall standing by itself between the firepit and the opening of the ventilation shaft. This deflector stone is thought to have prevented the draft of fresh air from blowing over the fire.

Recall now the inner features of the old Basketmaker III and Pueblo I pit houses. You can see that the final form of the kiva is the result of a slow, continual architectural development and is the best example of the amazing continuity of Anasazi forms throughout Anasazi history. The kiva in its larger form is the final expression of the old pit houses used originally by the early Anasazi.

As you examine the architectural detail of the kiva you can catch one of the few glimpses, thanks to the modern Pueblo, of something of the Anasazi people themselves. Along with rock art and visual images on pottery bowls, this is the closest understanding you may be afforded of the people who constructed these sites. In the symbolic forms and features of the kiva you see a little of the spiritual and inner view of the outside world—their world view, if you will—that forms a part of the character of the Anasazi and the modern Pueblo people.

Consider for a moment our own world view. The world is round. The moon is a body of rock that circles the earth every twenty-eight days, the earth circles the sun, the sun is part of a large

galaxy with uncountable other suns, and so on. This is our view of the physical world and we are certain that it is true. It tells us generally where we are in space and on earth at any given time, and usually defines our relationship with other places and often with other people.

For the Pueblo and most surely for the Anasazi, there was no such view. The earth was flat with mountains and canyons, and circular like a giant disc. All people lived on this construct and like us there was no sense of uncertainty about that and no real need to question. To be sure, the Anasazi recognized that beyond their circle or disc were great bodies of water, of interest in story and mythology but of no great daily importance. Further, this flat round surface was defined by the Pueblo and limited by four mountain peaks in the four directions that formed and enclosed the Pueblo world. All of life and the necessary resources for life and all things spiritual and practical were contained within a circle defined by these four peaks. The Anasazi recognized as do the Pueblo today two other directions, up and down, making six directions in all. Beneath this surface disc were three more "discs," one beneath the other that formed the other important parts of the world.

The enclosed circle of the four peaks was subdivided into a series of smaller concentric circles until the center of

the village was reached, for the Pueblo the central point of the world. In many pueblos and probably in many Anasazi sites, there is or was a center hole somewhere in the plaza that marks this point.

Just outside the village were four sacred points in the four directions that formed a circle around the village—where most Anasazi life took place. Within this village circle food was prepared, ceremonies performed, birth and death occurred, and most life was centered. This marks the second circle, the first being the center of the plaza.

A half mile or mile beyond the village, was often a set of circular stone structures, in some villages with a keyhole opening oriented to the center of the village. This formed the third circle, where fields were planted, hunting was done and much of daily farming activities took place. Beyond this circle is the final circle formed by the mountain peaks. Within this area hunting and gathering of other resources occurred—clays for pottery; wood for construction; game and plants for food, curing, and ceremonies. For a Pueblo and perhaps for the Anasazi, the closer you are to the center, that is the village, the better, happier, and more secure life will be. To leave the final outside circle is almost as unthinkable as it would be for us to leave earth itself.

The discs or worlds beneath the surface relate to the Pueblo spiritual world and the places of origin—for all people must account for how they got here and where they came from. And they must account for themselves in time, for preceding generations and how they acquired the knowledge to grow corn, make pottery, and perform the ceremonies necessary to keep the world functioning.

These Pueblo accounts or tales of origin serve the same purpose as our biblical story of Adam and Eve or, for a modern scientist, evolution. We have a choice of world views, but for the Anasazi and the Pueblo there is, or was, only one account that makes sense and that works.

The Pueblo origin story begins in the lowest of the four discs. The journey from this world to the next was made up a pole or log and through a small opening to the next surface above. To climb up a ladder and through the opening in the roof of the kiva is for Pueblo people a symbolic reenactment of this original journey. In time, following the same process and with the knowledge and assistance of other spiritual beings, the Anasazi "emerged" onto the surface as people.

The Pueblo, and probably the Anasazi, are and were constantly aware of these lower worlds and the journey their ancestors made from one to another to bring them where they are today. Though the Pueblo, Zuni, and Hopi are not in the exact places where they were prehistorically, they are not far from where they have been for more than 2,000 years—close to the center and close to the world beneath of their origin.

Now to the point of all of this and its relationship to architecture. Mesa Verde–style kivas reflect this Anasazi world and spiritual view, and the view itself accounts for the form and features in the kiva. Our understanding can only be in barest of form and outline, and the details of this symbolism in architecture are probably not available to us. But in outline the form of the kiva relates to this world view as follows. First the kiva is circular, as is the world. Second, kivas are always below ground to the degree the ground conditions will allow, symbolizing the lower spiritual worlds. In later periods and in some larger cliff sites the kiva may be built above the present surface of the ground

(sandstone is hard to dig in). But it will be enclosed by the rooms of the rest of the village to give it a below-ground appearance. Finally, a kiva, in Anasazi times, was always entered by ladder or pole from an opening in the roof. Every time you climb out of or enter a kiva you reenact the emergence to the earth or return to the disc below.

In the floor of many Anasazi kivas, especially at Mesa Verde, is a small hole, often lined with the neck of a pottery vessel, in a line between the firepit and the ventilation shaft and southern recess. Called the *shipap* or *sipapu*, this small opening recalls and gives symbolic access to the third world below and so on.

The keyhole shape of kivas must also relate to this world view, as do the six pilasters, recalling the six directions.

Leaving kivas now and returning to other rooms at a site, as you examine the rooms and determine their functions you will find that they are arranged in logical clusters of living room, storage room, one to three granaries, and a plaza in front of the rooms. By defining these clusters you can picture the household unit and determine the number of families that lived in the cliff site. It may help to draw a quick map of the site and label each of the rooms.

You may also note that some of the doors in rooms have been walled up and closed. One explanation, based on research at Hopi, is that access to storage rooms and granaries can only be by related sisters. If two sisters and their families live side by side, both can have access to a single storage room. If the sister should die or move and a non-related or less closely related family takes up occupancy of the room, the storage and granary access is walled off. You may have to examine the walls closely to locate these walled-in doorways. And if you have two living rooms with access to the same storage room, you may have two sisters living side by side.

Finally, another exercise that you can carry out at a site is to determine the order in which rooms and sections were built. If a family moved into a site and built a room or two, the walls and corners were usually "tied." That is, the stone of one wall was laid continuously with the other or at the corners to form a single consistent wall. If another room was attached to the first rooms, either as an expansion by the original family or by a different family, the walls were not bonded during the new construction. Therefore, if you examine the ends and corners of the walls you will see that some of them "abut" others. By following this pattern through the village, you can determine the sequence of room construction in a site. This will give you an architectural history of the ruin. Locating and defining these wall abutments will also help identify the different family room clusters.

Other Architectural Features

After an examination of the rooms and the ceramic artifacts littering the floor of a cliff site, you will find an enormous number of small, less obvious features of interest, some no longer understandable and others that are.

Often second- or even third-story rooms that have fallen and are no longer visible will be outlined by smoke blackening on the ceiling of a cave. Or if you look carefully you can find small amounts of plaster or clay adhering to the wall that will indicate the past presence of another room.

Near, below, or around the site small pecked indentations in the rock face are remains of small steps or hand and toe holds that were used to climb into the site and make access a little safer for children and old people. These can often be some distance from the ruin, but will almost always be there.

If you look at the floor of the site or the midden area in front, in addition to the numerous pottery and chipped stone fragments, you will find corn cobs, small pieces of squash rind, pinyon nut shells, cactus pads, and remains of other food items. Sometimes it is worth getting down on your hands and knees to inspect the surface for these small artifacts. Do not disturb the midden soil, however.

Small fragments of cordage are also common. Most of these are made from twisted and knotted yucca fibers. They are pieces from a host of nets, bags, sandals, and string or rope of various kinds used for various purposes. More rarely, cotton strands are also found or small pieces of woven clothing. If you look closely at some of the pieces of cord, the faint remains of red or other colors can be found.

One of the most common plant artifacts, again usually only in small pieces, are the individual strands of turkey feather blankets. The feathers are usually gone, eaten by insects, but the quill-wrapped cordage may still be there. Originally quite large, these probably served as blankets at night and as warm coats in winter. They must have been a common item of apparel for many Anasazi.

KAYENTA CLIFF SITES

Ceramics at Kayenta sites have already been described to some degree. The same type of ceramics found on surface sites will be in the cliff sites as well. In addition to pottery styles, the main difference between Mesa Verde Anasazi sites and Kayenta sites will be in architecture.

The Kayenta people rarely took the time and trouble to work the stone that they used for the walls of their rooms; less often did they level the floors of the caves. Masonry walls are built of roughly chipped stone with uneven edges and copious mortar to hold the stone together. Walls are usually one or at most two stones, thick with large chunks of rock pushed in to the mortar to make the walls more or less of even thickness. Chinking stones are used but rarely form a nice pattern along even courses as at Mesa Verde.

Circular kivas are not common, and in some sites kivas look very much like some of the living rooms. Except perhaps in size, kivas are hard to differentiate from living rooms.

Often Kayenta sites will have a room with three stone walls and a wattle-and-daub wall across the front, with a rectangular doorway near the center. As you enter the room, there will be a deflector perpendicular to the door and a low wall that extended from the deflector to attach to the front wall. This arrangement is called an entry box and is distinctive to Kayenta Anasazi sites.

A combination of fine black on white wares with an occasional colorful polychrome sherd or two and the scabby masonry with the use of wattle and daub will assure you that the site is Kayenta.

Rock Art

The subject of rock art and its many forms and varieties is too complex for this book. Many excellent books on the subject exist and you may want to purchase one before you visit backcountry sites. Rock art is not common or elaborate at sites of the Northern San Juan people. More may have existed than we find today, but they may have been on surfaces where erosion has removed most of them. At Kayenta sites and at other locations throughout the canyons, you will encounter figures of mountain sheep and large, square-shouldered figures wearing necklaces, earrings, and clothing. Lizards, snakes and many other forms are also found.

Some of the rock art has geometric designs, often concentric circles. These were probably symbolic and are difficult to interpret today.

Some rock art figures such as the ubiquitous Kokopelli can be somewhat understood, because the Hopi and perhaps other Pueblo people still make

kachina dolls of Kokopelli. He is usually a stick figure with a humped back and a flute, and in many of the representations he will have a phallus in

many different sizes and forms. The figure is shown standing, sitting, or laying on his back playing his flute and almost always has an obscene joyous whimsy about him that hints at Anasazi humor—just as humor is so much a part of Hopi and Pueblo people today.

CHAPTER EIGHT

Visiting Sites in the Four Corners

We have no accurate count of the number of known Anasazi sites within the Four Corners region, and probably thousands remain unrecorded and some even unknown. Based on the numbers of sites known from areas such as Mesa Verde or around Chaco, there are tens of thousands of Anasazi sites in the Four Corners alone. Further, even the number of the more prominent late Pueblo III cliff dwellings has never been calculated, but with some 600 to 700 in Mesa Verde National Park alone, 300 to 400 in Grand Gulch, and similar numbers in Canyon de Chelly, Canyonlands, and other locations in the Southwest, there are probably thousands of these types of sites as well. The same can be said of Pueblo II villages, rock art sites and panels, and a seemingly infinite number and variety of towers, pit houses, and other remains.

This section of the book will list some of the backcountry areas that lend themselves to access and visitation by the general public. Only general areas will be described. The specific location of individual sites will usually not be discussed. This book should be viewed as a beginning point for those who wish to explore Anasazi sites, not as a detailed guide. For specific information consult federal or other offices listed at the back or other personal and official sources.

Most locations are on federal lands, but many others can be found on state or even county lands. Private lands usually do not lend themselves to public use, but there are some exceptions. In the Four Corners area state and private lands are often intermingled with federal land, especially BLM land. But unless these private lands are fenced or signed, it is usually permissible to wander freely on them.

Many portions of National Park Service (NPS) and Indian lands are not open to the public. Before exploring NPS or tribal lands, it is essential that you inquire. In some cases, such as on the Navajo Reservation, certain areas are open for visitation and hiking by the public with a proper permit. On others, such as the Ute Homelands in southwestern Colorado, access is generally forbidden. Backcountry permits are often required in NPS areas as well.

A number of map sources are available to the public that will help locate which areas are open and which are not. The U. S. Forest Service and the Bureau of Land management sell excellent maps of their areas. These maps will generally show federal lands, common roads, and private lands within the forests. These maps are available from local Forest Service and BLM offices in the four-state region. Finally, the best source of map information remains the topographic maps from the U.S. Geological Survey. These maps provide detailed information on land features, topography, road locations, and other information for those hiking or driving in the backcountry. These maps can be purchased from the USGS in Denver or from sporting goods stores and many other locations in towns throughout the Four Corners area.

National Park Service Areas

The major National Park Service areas are generally well known and most of them have been referenced previously in this book. These areas, most of which are reached by paved highways, should be the beginning point for any visitor to Anasazi ruins in the Four Corners area. Nearly all of the ruins in these parks require a hike of varying distances and varying degrees of difficulty.

Mesa Verde National Park and Chaco Culture National Historical Park are two that should not be missed. Mesa Verde has an enormous number of ruins representing most of the different periods of Anasazi occupation from Basketmaker III pit houses to the largest and most spectacular Pueblo III cliff dwelling in the Southwest. It also has one of the best, most in-depth museums of any of the National Park Service's archaeological areas. The park requires from one to three days to properly visit.

Major ruins available to the public are found on two of the dozen or so mesas in the park—the Chapin and Wetherill Mesa complexes. Each requires the better part of a day to visit. In addition, longer hikes and a half-day horseback trip are usually possible. Mesa Verde can be visited and revisited any number of times with new things to find each time. The largest cliff dwellings in the Southwest are located here at Cliff Palace, Long House, and Spruce Tree House. These housed up to 300 or 400 people with some fifteen to twenty kivas in each site. Surface ruins include ceremonial complexes at Sun Temple, examples of water control reservoirs such as Mummy Lake, and a number of other smaller features. Even with all this, only some 10 to 15 percent of the ruins in the park have been excavated and are open to the public, with hundreds of others in the backcountry parts of the park. Mesa Verde is one of the primary locations of the Northern San Juan Anasazi population.

Chaco Culture National Historical Park is located in northwestern New Mexico. Like Mesa Verde it was one of the centers of Anasazi culture. It is the headquarters, if you will, of the Chaco expansion in the late 1000s and early 1100s and contains some of the largest, standing, open villages in the Southwest. Backcountry trips to some of the outlying ruins are possible with

a permit from the park and there is an opportunity to see some of the more interesting rock art, stairways cut in sandstone cliffs that were part of the road system, and other interesting features. Park personnel can recommend other short trips near and in the park.

A great deal of literature is available on these two parks as well as dozens of recent books and other publications. The reader should consult some of this literature before visiting these and other Four Corners parks.

Other NPS areas in the Four Corners that are equally interesting and relatively accessible are Aztec Ruins, Navajo National Monument, and Canyon de Chelly. Of the three, only Aztec Ruins is available for detailed exploration without major hiking or jeep expeditions. All require some time to visit. The ruins at Navajo National Monument, part of the Kayenta Anasazi, are all essentially backcountry sites that can be reached only by long hikes or horseback rides. They are situated in some of the most beautiful red sandstone canyon country in the Southwest. Keet Seel is an eight-mile, one-way hike or horseback ride and Betatakin is a half-day trip by foot. The third ruin, Inscription House, has been closed to the public for a number of years and may or may not be opened in the future.

Canyon de Chelly contains dozens of

major cliff ruins as well as scores of smaller earlier sites in one of the most spectacular sandstone canyons in the Four Corners. Access to the ruins is by jeep only except for a hike down to White House Ruin from the rim of the canyon. Many of the ruins in the monument can be viewed from the roads above the canyons. Although guided hikes into the lower reaches of the monument are available, backcounrry hiking or general wandering are not allowed because the canyons are still home to many Navajo families. Canyon de Chelly and its companion canyons contain Anasazi sites from Basketmaker II through Pueblo IV. It is a fascinating and important center of Anasazi culture. Ruins in the canyon reflect both Northern San Juan Anasazi culture and Chaco people, although no great kivas or other elaborate remains of the Chaco outliers are found here.

Less well-known NPS areas invite the more adventurous, and some lend themselves to extended backcountry hiking and river experiences.

Hovenweep National Monument in southwestern Colorado and southeastern Utah is at the center of a group of very late Pueblo III canyon rim sites. Some of these are included in the monument and others are on nearby BLM land. Seeing them all can combine some of the the best short hikes and dirt road trips to sites anywhere in the

Four Corners. The monument and nearby BLM lands are filled with ruins of nearly all time periods of Anasazi development except for the rare Basketmaker II sites. The monument contains several detached units with examples of exceptional architecture. These can be reached by rough roads; some may require four-wheel drive. Hovenweep can serve as a central point for visiting sites such as Hackberry, Horseshoe, and Cutthroat Castle, as well as some of the better known BLM sites such as McClain Basin Towers, Pedro Point Ruin, Cannonball Mesa, and Lowry Ruins. Backcountry camping is available on BLM lands, or more developed camping facilities are available at the monument.

In southeastern Utah at Canyonlands National Park and Natural Bridges National Monument are numerous Anasazi ruins that are accessible to only the most committed backpacker and desert wanderer. Natural Bridges offers day hikes to some interesting and less-well-understood late Pueblo III ruins in White Canyon.

The best of the backcountry ruins are in Canyonlands, a park where the archaeology is only beginning to be charted and understood. Canyonlands is basically a backpacking, hiking, and rough-road park with some of the most remote and classic canyon, slickrock, and mesa lands in the Southwest. Most

archaeological sites can only be reached by four-wheel drive or on foot. The park contains dozens of undisturbed late Pueblo III cliff dwellings perched high in caves in cliffs. In addition, there are some of the finest examples of Indian rock art to be found in this country, including both Anasazi and Fremont styles. It is also a park where ruins are still occasionally found by the public, and where many sites remain unrecorded and undocumented. The Salt Creek drainage and Horse Creek in the Needles District are two good locations, but sites are likely to be encountered in many other places. Canyonlands is also a good place to visit sites along the Colorado and Green rivers.

Glen Canyon National Recreation Area, also in southeastern Utah, contains some of the finest examples of late Pueblo III Kayenta architecture to be found. The ruins, mostly cliff dwellings, are found in a number of side canyons where the sites were originally well above the water level of Lake Powell. Many sites were destroyed in the mid-1960s when the canyons were flooded to create the lake. Remaining sites contain excellent examples of wattle-and-daub construction in a form typical of the Kayenta culture, as well as original roofs and other well-preserved architectural features. Some fine large pictographs also exist within the area. Boating within the maze of narrow sandstone canyons can be a lovely experience despite the presence of motorboats and other noisy creatures. Besides, archaeology need not always be hard work. It often goes well with the relaxation of a house boat and a warm canyon sun.

In total, National Park Service areas offer a broad array of experiences with archaeology. Park areas also have the advantage of providing a great deal of information about the area, its ruins, and the archaeology of the Anasazi. Some park museums have good interpretive exhibits as well.

Bureau of Land Management Areas

Lands managed by the U.S. Bureau of Land Management (BLM) contain many backcountry archaeological sites and offer spectacular canyon scenery as well. This agency, which is nearly unknown in the East, manages most of the public lands in the West, primarily those lands that were deemed unsuitable for homesteads, parks, or other uses. As you travel through the vast expanses of the West by car, most of the mesa and desert lands between Denver and Reno are BLM lands. Though many consider them "waste lands," these public lands have beautiful areas that are as lovely

as many of the parks. They are less well known, less well advertised, and require more effort to visit. It's an adventure well worth the trouble.

BLM lands contain the bulk of remaining Anasazi and other archaeological sites. They are the great repositories of prehistoric remains left in the American West. But it takes a great deal more sleuthing to find locations to visit. The bureau has limited recreational and cultural resource programs and generally neither encourages nor discourages public use. Information can be found in bureau offices in towns throughout the Four Corners, from the archaeological literature, and by word of mouth. One of the greatest benefits for the backcountry traveler, whether on foot or in an old pickup truck, is that all BLM lands are open to the public. One can wander freely and usually encounter few people along the way.

It is impossible to list all the areas that contain archaeological remains of interest. We will here highlight only a few, but as you visit them you will learn of many others. In recent years the BLM has excavated and stabilized a number of Anasazi sites in southwestern Colorado and southeastern Utah that are easily accessible.

In southwestern Colorado the bureau operates an excellent museum, the Anasazi Heritage Center, with extensive new exhibits reflecting much of

our current view of Anasazi archaeology. This large facility near Dolores, Colorado, houses more than two million archaeological specimens and promises to become a major resource in the Four Corners region. Near the center is a stabilized ruin, Escalante Ruin, a major Chaco outlier. The site offers an unparalled view of the Northern San Juan Anasazi area. Near Escalante Ruin is a small four-room site, the Dominguez Ruin, that yielded one of the few high-status burials known from southwestern Colorado. In addition to a beautiful turquoise and shell frog pendant, the burial of a young woman contained almost 7,000 jet and shell beads that had been strung originally into several strands to make an elaborate necklace.

In addition to Escalante, the BLM manages a large open site, Lowry Ruins, west of Pleasant View, Colorado. This site was one of the early excavations in the Four Corners and has been stabilized for public use. It is part of one of the large central towns that the Anasazi constructed in Montezuma Valley and one that was also involved with the Chaco phenomenon. Additional excavations are underway at another part of the town by the Fort Lewis College summer field school program.

Beyond these developed sites, most sites on BLM lands in southwestern Colorado can by all rights be called backcountry ruins. They require at a minimum driving over rough dirt roads and hiking to reach most of them. As previously mentioned, some of the most spectacular late Pueblo III sites can be visited in conjunction with the Hovenweep sites and are from the same general time period; for the most part they have not been stabilized or excavated. Other sites lay on the half dozen or so mesas and canyons west of the extensive bean fields around Dove Creek, Colorado. Information on visiting these ruins should be sought from the BLM office in Durango, Colorado.

These prehistoric sites along the western edge of southwestern Colorado present an almost full range of Anasazi culture history. The area contains Basketmaker III pit house villages and numerous examples of the Pueblo II unit type villages, as well as examples of the very large long-term central villages such as Lowry Pueblo, Cannonball Village, and Seven Tower Ruin. The architecturally interesting complexes of towers and smaller villages typical of the last period of occupation are also well represented in this area. Missing, for the most part, are the Pueblo I sites, the period when the southwestern Colorado people moved to higher areas along the Dolores River and into other similar locations. Also unknown in this region are Basketmaker II sites. Areas to inquire about are Cahone Mesa, Cannonball Mesa, Negro Canyon, Sand Canyon, and Yellow Jacket Canyon.

The bureau is currently developing a hiking trail through one of the canyons near Cortez called Sand Canyon that will provide access to both the large Sand Canyon Pueblo being excavated by the Crow Canyon Archaeological Center and dozens of small cliff dwellings found in the canyon. It will be an excellent one- or two-day canyon hiking adventure.

While the BLM sites in southwestern Colorado contain an enormous number of Anasazi sites, southeastern Utah is probably the richest in backcountry sites and accompanying spectacular landscapes. It has a further advantage in being less settled. Many BLM lands in southeastern Utah could easily become part of the national park system because of their scenic, environmental, and archaeological resources. It is also here that the best preservation of archaeological materials are found, with some of the best examples of perishable artifacts and some of the finest rock art remains. One could pursue lands almost forever and still not exhaust this region.

The BLM in Utah has also excavated and stabilized a number of large late Pueblo III sites. Some of these, like Mule Canyon Ruins along Highway 95 west of Blanding and Big Westwater Ruin south of Blanding, are within easy reach of the highway and provide good examples of the later occupations of Northern San Juan Anasazi in this area.

In addition, the state of Utah is also very active in the preservation of several important sites for public use. An excellent museum is located at the Edge of the Cedars State Historical Park in Blanding. The museum contains a large collection of Anasazi ceramic artifacts from a local collection as well as a large Pueblo II surface site. This site, although only partly excavated, is a large central village like Lowry and also seems to have influences from Chaco Canyon. It may represent the westernmost expansion of the Chaco intrusion into the Northern San Juan Anasazi culture area, although the extension of Chaco culture into southeast Utah is still largely unresearched.

There are two major backcountry areas on BLM lands in Utah that hold exciting archaeological adventures. They are the Grand Gulch Primitive Area and the Ruin Park/Beef Basin area.

Grand Gulch reportedly derives its name from a comment by an early Mormon cowboy, who on first seeing the canyon said that it was certainly a Grand Canyon, and was told that one of those already existed. He replied, "Then it is one hell of a Grand Gulch." An appropriate description of the place. Grand Gulch is an elaborate system of canyons cut into the western end of Cedar Mesa, an extensive, flat, pinyon-covered mesa above the San Juan River very much a Utah version of the Mesa Verde. The entire Cedar Mesa area is densely covered with Anasazi ruins from both the Kayenta and Northern San Juan Anasazi groups. Along the mesa tops are sites from Pueblo II and early Pueblo III time periods as well as occasional Basketmaker III pit house sites. In Grand Gulch and the other canyons that drain into the San Juan River are numerous cliff dwellings from the Pueblo III period. Many examples of Basketmaker III and early Pueblo I sites are located on ridges and sand dunes in the canyons and along the lower mesa areas. Grand Gulch itself is one of a half dozen centers of Basketmaker II development. It is one of the few areas where Basketmaker II sites can be recognized on the surface in caves and other locations which often contain later Pueblo III masonry structures.

Trips to Grand Gulch and the tributary canyons involve at least a day's hike into the canyon from the few points along the rim accessible by vehicle. Most trips into the area involve backpacking for a minimum of several days. The BLM maintains a backcountry ranger station at Kane Gulch on Cedar Mesa, and information about the canyon is available from BLM offices in Monticello or Moab, Utah.

The Beef Basin and Ruin Park regions can be reached from the entry road to the Needles District of Canyonlands National Park. Many of these sites, which consist of large open villages of Pueblo II and Pueblo III time, with substantial masonry, can be reached by four-wheel-drive vehicles along this road. The area is fairly dense with pinyon and juniper and provides excellent camping as well as an opportunity to visit the various ruins along the way. Again, general information is available from the BLM offices mentioned above.

In addition to these better known and more clearly defined areas of BLM land in southeastern Utah, the region is cut by scores of smaller canyons, and contains many small buttes and mesas that are also rich in archaeological sites and rock art. These are more difficult to reach and even in some cases to find. But with a little research and familiarity with the country, they are accessible.

A special archaeological treat is a trip on the San Juan River in the area of Bluff, Utah. Large panels of elaborate pictographs and petroglyphs are found along the banks of the river as well as a number of Pueblo I and later Pueblo III cliff sites. The San Juan is not as hazardous as the stretches of the Colorado in Canyonlands. While it is not a river for the amateur, it can be negotiated by a reasonably experienced group.

Commercial trips on the San Juan, one of the lesser known, less crowded, and more beautiful southwestern rivers, are available. Check in Bluff for companies, some of which specialize in archaeological trips.

In addition to the sites along the river itself, with an additional day or two a hiking trip up from the mouth of the Chinle (the same river and canyon that begins at Canyon de Chelly) allows access to some of the least visited sites in the Four Corners. The Chinle also contains outstanding rock art, especially later Navajo petroglyphs, and a number of cliff sites and smaller surface ruins. It is a delightful backcountry hike.

Further removed from general knowledge are hundreds of other sites in locations in the desert country of Utah on BLM or state lands. A few to search for are Ceremonial Mesa, Seven Window House, the Nancy Patterson Site, Cottonwood Canyon sites, Comb Ridge sites and cliff trails, Recapture Wash and Montezuma Canyon ruins, Bubble Cave, and a lovely spot known only to one old grizzled desert rat, the Potholes. Many of these areas involve simply hiking and encountering ruins as they may occur.

Some of the finest, most remote, and best backpacking can be found in the small canyons that drain into Comb Wash from the west—Arch Canyon,

Owl Canyon, Fish Creek, and Mule Canyon. These delightful canyons, small versions of Grand Gulch, offer the essence of southwestern canyon backpacking. Each canyon contains Pueblo III cliff dwellings, rock art, and eden-like pools. A trip into these canyons by the more adventurous is well worth the effort. Further information can be obtained at local BLM offices.

Much of northwestern New Mexico is part of the Navajo Indian Reservation and will be discussed later in the section on Navajo backcountry archaeology. BLM lands in northwestern New Mexico are found to the north of the San Juan and east of the reservation. Most interesting archaeologically is the Gobernador area. This is a region of unique sites from the Pueblo IV period. The masonry structures here were constructed following the successful rebellion by the Rio Grande Pueblos against the Spanish in 1680. Fearing an immediate return and fierce retribution, several groups of Pueblos moved north into the Gobernador region and built shelters that have the same defensive character as late Pueblo III sites in the Four Corners. They also contain different architectural features, such as corner fireplaces and other items of Spanish culture. The BLM office in Farmington can provide information necessary to visit these sites.

Less obvious but of great interest are the Chaco sites and remnants of the Chaco road system that traverse BLM and Navajo lands north of Chaco Canyon. A well-researched and planned trip to some of these remains is an inspiring venture for the true archaeological aficionado.

Forest Service Sites

U.S. Forest Service lands in the Four Corners have somewhat fewer Anasazi sites than BLM lands because most Forest Service lands are at elevations above the Anasazi farming and living areas. However, significant archaeological remains are found on forest lands in all four states in the lower elevations. A few of these have been developed, but most remain as backcountry sites.

One of the most spectacular settings for an Anasazi site in the Four Corners is Chimney Rock Pueblo. Located in southwestern Colorado near Pagosa Springs, it is one of the easternmost Anasazi sites in Colorado. Referred to as the Machu Picchu of the Southwest, the ruin is located along a narrow ridge on a high promontory above the Piedra River valley where ponderosa pine and pinyon zones meet. The Chimney Rocks are two rock spires visible for many miles around.

This ruin consists of a large Chaco outlier masonry room block with a series of unusual circular masonry structures and a great kiva. Many portions of the site have not been excavated. Several intriguing explanations for the site's different architecture and eastern location have been offered. Recent research has suggested that at least one function of the Chaco road and outlier system was to haul the 200,000-odd beams into Chaco Canyon for the large communities. Chimney Rock would have been an excellent source for the beams although no details are presently known. Guided tours of Chimney Rock are conducted in the summer by special arrangement with the Forest Service office in Pagosa Springs.

Besides this one developed site, there are many more Anasazi ruins on Forest Service lands. Most can be found in central and southern Arizona, although Forest Service areas in Utah also contain a number of interesting Anasazi sites. An area known as Elk Ridge in Utah, at a slightly higher elevation than the surrounding desert, seems to have been another Pueblo I refugium or relocation area for the Anasazi between A.D. 700 and A.D. 900. In the Santa Fe, Carson, and other forests in New Mexico are scores of sites from the Gallina Culture of the Anasazi and a number of large to very large ruins from the Pueblo IV and so-called Refugee Period of Anasazi culture. Many of these sites can be the focus for excellent back-country trips. For further information on sites open to the public, contact any Forest Service office in the Four Corners region.

Ute Tribal Park

The Ute Mountain Ute Tribal Park is located just south of Mesa Verde National Park. Although complete surveys have not been done, it has been estimated that at least as many prehistoric sites exist on the Ute lands to the south as are found within Mesa Verde National Park.

Hundreds of cliff dwellings and surface sites, some quite large, exist on Ute lands. A decade or so ago the Ute Mountain Ute Tribe sponsored the excavation and stabilization of some of the larger cliff ruins and have made them available for visitors. Three of the larger Pueblo III cliff sites, Johnson Ruin, Lion House, and Hoy House, can be visited as part of a tour conducted by members of the Ute tribe. It is an opportunity to see not only these sites but also a very different view of the Mesa Verde from the south, and to realize the full area the Anasazi used and occupied. Tours can be arranged through the Ute Mountain Tribe in Towaoc; this is an interesting back-country trip.

Ute lands generally are not open to archaeologists or the public. Understandably, the Utes are most reluctant to have people wandering on their lands, and they themselves tend to avoid the sites. This is an area, and certainly we need a few of them, that is likely to remain undeveloped and unknown for many years to come.

Navajo and Hopi Lands

Nearly all of Arizona in the Four Corners region is part of the large Navajo Indian Reservation. And nearly all Navajo lands contain prehistoric remains of the Anasazi. The Hopi Reservation, which is surrounded by the Navajo Reservation, is also rich in Anasazi sites. There is almost no part of either reservation that does not contain village remains both large and small. All the time periods and types of sites in the complete range of Anasazi prehistory are represented, from Basketmaker II sites in the northern areas to Pueblo IV. In the Hopi villages Pueblo V, or modern Pueblo, occupation continues. Three previously mentioned National Park Service areas, Chaco Canyon, Canyon de Chelly, and Navajo National Monument, are found on these lands in northeastern Arizona. Beyond these park areas and one village administered by the Navajo tribe are

thousands of other Anasazi sites. All qualify as backcountry ruins and require considerable knowledge and effort to locate and visit.

Archaeological sites on Navajo and other Indian lands are protected by federal, state, and tribal laws. Navajo rangers patrol the backcountry of the reservation to enforce the laws.

Visiting ruins requires a permit from the Navajo Tribe at its headquarters in Window Rock. You should contact the tribe by letter or phone requesting a permit to visit these areas. There is usually a charge for the permits.

Though the Hopi at present have no formal permit system for visiting ruins on their lands, it is generally a good idea to contact the tribal government for permission and information to locate the sites.

Because Navajo and Hopi live here, it is essential that courtesy and common sense govern visits to these areas. Stay clear of homes and hogan areas and avoid interference with livestock on the reservations. Finally, it is probably easier to get stuck in the sandy Navajo desert than any other place on earth so some knowledge of desert driving, good equipment, and good vehicles are also essential.

A little time spent on these lands can result in a greater understanding and awareness of the Hopi and the Navajo and some lasting friendships. You will also be introduced to the diversity and beauty of Navajo and Hopi culture. A number of pleasant surprises are in store for those who take advantage of these opportunities.

The ruins and areas listed below are some of the better known and more frequently visited areas on the reservations. However, remember that nearly all of these lands contain Anasazi ruins that are not as well known but are as interesting and exciting.

Two major archaeological areas on Navajo lands are basically extensions of two National Park Service areas. These are the Defiance Plateau and Chinle Wash extending out from Canyon de Chelly and the Tsegi Canyon/Navajo Mountain area, an extension of Navajo National Monument.

From Kayenta, Arizona, north to the Colorado River the Navajo Reservation is an incredible maze of canyons and mesas—too many even to attempt to name. It must have been one of the most remote and difficult areas for the Anasazi to travel. But no part of this area is without ruins. Between Navajo National Monument and Navajo Mountain is the Tsegi Canyon system, one of the centers of the Kayenta Anasazi. Tsegi and its branch canyons, the Dogozibito, Long, Keet Seel, and Nagashi Biken, contain numerous sites as do the mesas above—Skeleton Mesa, Hoskinni Mesa, and Shonto Plateau.

There are no roads in these canyons and some of the mesas are roadless as well. Only a few points of access exist, of which Navajo National Monument is one.

Permits to backpack and hike in the Tsegi system are available from the Navajo Tribe, and additional information can be obtained at Navajo National Monument.

Even more remote are the side canyons leading directly to the Colorado River from the flanks of Navajo Mountain. The mountain is one of the more prominent features of the reservation and is sacred to the Navajo. Access to the mountain and some of the side canyons is forbidden. However, there are a number of beautiful areas to visit, both with and without archaeological sites. A good beginning is the hike from Navajo Mountain to Rainbow Bridge.

West of the Tsegi system and Navajo Mountain is the even larger and more remote Navajo Canyon system. It was occupied by the Kayenta Anasazi as were the Kaibito and Rainbow plateaus above; little more is known of the region. Many of the side canyons along what is now Lake Powell in Glen Canyon National Recreation Area were surveyed many years ago, and a large number of sites, many flooded by the lake, were recorded. These areas combined provide an area for backpacking and backroad exploration to satisfy even the

most experienced and most intensely interested public. Again, information about the area and permits should be obtained from the Navajo Tribe.

Chinle Wash flows north in an almost straight line for approximately sixty miles from the mouth of Canyon de Chelly until it empties into the San Juan River in Utah, just west of Bluff. The Chinle was continuously occupied by Anasazi throughout its length and contains one of the largest cliff dwellings in Arizona. There are few roads within the drainage itself although there are numerous points of access on either side. Many Navajos live here and permits must be acquired from the tribe before visiting any of the areas or archaeological sites in the canyon. You will almost certainly be asked for one by the Navajos who reside there.

The one large site, Poncho House, frequently shown on popular maps of the area, is a fascinating Anasazi cliff site. Unfortunately it has not been stabilized and has been subjected to severe vandalism and pothunting. It is very fragile, and massive damage is imminent unless badly needed repair and stabilization are done. One should be extremely careful when visiting this site and should be on the lookout for pothunters in the area.

Monument Valley is one of the few areas on the Navajo Reservation that is well known to the general population.

Many people have visited the valley or at least seen it in movies or television ads. It has almost become a caricature of the American Southwest with red sandstone buttes, mesa remnants, and spires. One of the loveliest places in America, it is also rich in Anasazi remains. Much of the valley is a part of the Navajo Tribal Park and is patrolled by the Navajo Tribal Rangers. Access to the park, much like national park areas, is limited and fairly carefully controlled.

Visits to Monument Valley and its archaeological remains are generally by jeep. Trips can be arranged at tribal park headquarters, and groups are usually accompanied by a Navajo ranger. Accommodations and private jeep trips can also be arranged through the historic Goulding's Trading Post. Though Monument Valley may not be open for general hiking and backpacking, it is one area that should be on your list. Sites are also from the Kayenta Anasazi, and the valley contains a number of late Pueblo III cliff dwellings as well as other smaller Basketmaker III and Pueblo II ruins. A number of roads lead into other parts of the valley, usually to Navajo communities; several, however, lead to secluded archaeological sites. A permit is required from the Navajo Tribe.

Backcountry trips to archaeological remains on Navajo lands obviously require more planning than the average southwestern visitor is accustomed to. More time and effort are required to explore some of these areas. As previously mentioned, the Navajo Tribe neither encourages nor forbids visitation to its lands, but it does wish to maintain control; hence, permits for specific areas are needed, federal and Navajo laws must be obeyed, and the Navajo people must not be subjected to scrutiny and intrusion. It's a small price for the many exciting places and ruins that are available on Navajo lands.

Hopi Lands and Sites

In addition to the many Kayenta Anasazi sites on Black Mesa and other parts of the Hopi Reservation, there are two extremely interesting and historically important sites at Hopi. Neither are formally open for visitation to the public, but permission to visit can be arranged with the Hopi Tribal Office on Second Mesa. One is the ruins of the village of Awatovi. Awatovi was occupied historically by the Hopi and back into the Pueblo III era of Anasazi prehistory. When the Spaniards arrived at Hopi in the early 1600s, they constructed a church at Awatovi and one at Oraibi. During the Pueblo Rebellion in 1680, the priest at Awatovi was killed and his church destroyed. The Hopi in other villages thought that the people at Awatovi had been too co-

operative with the Spaniards, or for other reasons we may never know, the community was burned by the Hopi themselves. The site was excavated in part by Harvard's Peabody Museum, and some of the finest colorful kiva murals of Hopi religious figures and symbols were recorded.

A second site is Sityatki on First Mesa. Partially excavated during the early part of this century, it is one of the classic Pueblo IV villages in the Four Corners and was occupied just prior to some of the modern Pueblo villages.

A final location of major archaeological remains on Navajo and Hopi lands is on Black Mesa just south of Navajo National Monument and to the north of the Hopi villages. Black Mesa is the site of the immense Peabody Coal Company strip mine which in itself is a "site" to behold. A great deal is known about the archaeology of Black Mesa as a result of excavations conducted to mitigate damage from the mining. It too was a center of Kayenta Anasazi and exhibits a full range of archaeological sites, including numerous Basketmaker II sites. Most of the remaining sites are surface ruins and villages dating to Pueblo II and III times, though few Pueblo III cliff dwellings are found. Along the southern edge of the mesa are Pueblo IV sites ancestral to the existing Hopi villages.

Black Mesa is a good place to examine surface ruins. Much of Black Mesa is in the disputed zone between the Hopi and Navajo reservations. Tension and hostility currently run high over this issue and probably will for many years to come. Certainly a permit is necessary to visit Black Mesa and care should be exercised in visiting the area.

A visit to Hopi should also include, at a minimum, a visit to the village of Old Oraibi. Based on minimal archaeological testing of the village middens and the recovery of datable house beams, Oraibi is the oldest continuously occupied community in America.

And finally, a trip to Hopi is also an opportunity to acquaint yourself with a nearly intact old culture. Throughout the summer and fall months the Hopi frequently perform various kachina ceremonies and other rituals associated with their religion and agricultural needs. The public is welcome to many of these ceremonials. The combination of centuries-old music, drama, satire, and costumes seen at Hopi today probably occurred in a somewhat similar form in Kayenta Anasazi villages to the north 700 years ago. Visiting Hopi and talking with Hopi people can provide an entirely different understanding of Anasazi people than that provided by books.

Zuni Lands and Sites

While perhaps outside our somewhat arbitrarily defined Four Corners country, a few comments about sites at Zuni are in order. The present village of Zuni, or Halona as it is also called, dates from just after the Pueblo Rebellion. Zuni is one of the Seven Cities of Cibola sought by the first Spaniards who entered what is now the United States in 1539. Fray Marcos de Niza and his group viewed, and some members of his party visited, the village of Hawikuh near Zuni. It was this trip that ultimately resulted in the Spanish settlement of New Mexico, as well as Texas and California. The ruins of Hawikuh are not far from the present village of Zuni as are the ruins of Yellow House and several other Pueblo IV communities. Arrangements to visit these and other sites can be made in Zuni at the Zuni Tribal Headquarters.

State and County Sites

Generally the Four Corners states do not have substantial lands with archaeological sites. However, some interesting developed archaeological sites may be visited. One mentioned previously is Edge of the Cedars State Historical Park near Blanding, Utah. The state of Utah also manages two other sites of interest. Newspaper Rock State Park contains a large, complicated petroglyph panel. It is along the road to the Needles District of Canyonlands National Park. A second archaeological park in southern Utah is the Anasazi Indian Village State Historical Monument near Boulder, Utah. This is an excellent example of the Virgin River or Western Kayenta Anasazi branch.

One of the major Chaco sites in the Four Corners, Salmon Ruins near Farmington, New Mexico, is operated by San Juan County as a public archaeological park. Partially excavated in the 1970s, Salmon is the terminus of the great Northern Road from Chaco Canyon. The county also has an excellent museum and research facility near the site. Salmon is a good site to visit in conjunction with a visit to Chaco Canyon and Aztec Ruins and could well serve as the beginning or ending point for a backcountry trip along the great Northern Road to Chaco.

Many small communities in the Four Corners have county historical museums of varying quality. Nearly all have in their collections archaeological material that has been donated. Many have excellent individual pieces that are well worth a trip to the museum. For example, the museum in Telluride, Colorado, has one of the largest and finest pieces of prehistoric decorated cotton blanket in existence.

Privately Owned Sites

There are many large, spectacular, and interesting Anasazi sites on private lands. Many, if not most, of the largest Pueblo II and Pueblo III villages in southwestern Colorado are on private lands. Efforts are underway to purchase and donate a number of the larger ones to public bodies such as the National Park Service, BLM, and local colleges. Access to these sites is, of course, only with the permission of the landowner. The willingness of owners to allow visitors varies widely.

Several important sites that would be worth some inquiry are the Yellow Jacket Site north of Cortez, Colorado, and the Wallace Ruin, Ida Jean, and the so-called Toltec Ruin west of Cortez. The Yellow Jacket site contains an estimated 1,820 rooms, 166 kivas, a great kiva, four distinct plazas, twenty tower remnants, and a fully developed community water system. It is the largest Anasazi site yet known in the Four Corners. It is a fascinating site to visit and one that should be in public ownership.

A good source of information on sites are local museums like the Heritage Center in Cortez, the Edge of the Cedars in Utah, and Salmon Ruins in Farmington. The Office of the State Archaeologist in any of the four states or local archaeological societies can also provide information on interesting private sites.

Other Anasazi Areas and Prehistoric Cultures

Three other areas or branches of the Anasazi Culture have been defined by archaeologists. These are the Virgin River Anasazi, the Little Colorado Anasazi, and the Rio Grande Anasazi. Because they are not as easily visited and not in the Four Corners area where the availability of backcountry sites is so much greater, consideration of them here will be brief.

The Virgin River Anasazi, also called the Western Kayenta Anasazi, occupied an area north of the Grand Canyon in north-central Arizona, extending well into western and southern Utah to the tip of Nevada. The Virgin River Anasazi are similar in many ways to the Kayenta peoples. They have similar architecture and similar but much less elaborate ceramics. A major distinguishing characteristic is an apparent lack of formalized kivas or other ritual architecture. Recent research has also included the so-called Sinagua Culture found to the north of Flagstaff, Arizona, in and around Wupatki National Monument, as a part of the Western Kayenta Anasazi branch. These peoples had, in late Pueblo II and early Pueblo III times, quite large, well-constructed, multistoried masonry villages; they also combined Kayenta Anasazi black on white and polychrome ceramics with a very different red and black ceramic style.

They would seem to be one of several variants of the overall Anasazi cultural tradition.

The Rio Grande branch is much better known, much more extensive, and of considerable importance to the overall Anasazi culture. In general, in the earlier periods from Basketmaker II through Pueblo III, their development follows that of the Four Corners Anasazi. Population was far less dense in the Rio Grande area, and Basketmaker III, Pueblo I, and Pueblo II sites are less common. Basketmaker II sites are rare. The Pueblo III period lacks some of the distinctive architecture found to the north, but many sites from that time period have been located. Examples are the Forked Lightning site near Pecos National Monument, sites in Bandelier National Monument, the Arroyo Hondo site east of Santa Fe, and Pot Creek near Taos. Most of these Pueblo III sites contain evidence of fairly large villages during the Pueblo II period as well. Major Anasazi or pre-Pueblo sites are also located in the Galisteo Basin, the Estancia Valley, and south along the Rio Grande, almost to Texas.

Rio Grande Anasazi cultural development is unique in that the succeeding Anasazi periods—Pueblo IV and Pueblo V—are more fully represented in the Rio Grande area than in the Four Corners region. It is also here that many of the remnants of the

Northern San Juan and Chaco people may have resettled. Many of the modern pueblos such as Acoma, Cochiti, and Taos are in the same location as earlier Rio Grande Anasazi sites and, as at Hopi, demonstrate continuous habitation from at least the twelfth century. The precise antiquity of these modern Pueblos is not known at present, but many were in use at least as early as the Pueblo III period. Other Pueblo villages were occupied when Spaniards entered the Southwest in the 1540s, but were abandoned just before or shortly after the Pueblo Rebellion of 1680. These include the seven large pueblos in the Galisteo Basin and the large villages of Gran Quivira, Abo, and Quairi in central New Mexico, as well as Hawikuh, Zuni, and Pecos.

The history and prehistory of the Rio Grande Anasazi are complex; it is such an important part of the cultural history of the Anasazi that a separate book is needed to describe it and to provide a guide to the many sites in this region available to the visiting public. Therefore, we will not attempt to examine the Rio Grande Anasazi and the later Pueblo periods in any further detail.

The third branch is the Little Colorado Anasazi, so named because they occupied the area drained by the Little Colorado River just south and east of Grand Canyon National Park. Although named as a branch of the Anasazi, they are less well-known than any other Anasazi groups. There is a growing body of information about this area, but its exact nature and relationship to other Anasazi and to the Mogollon people farther south is not well understood. There are a few interesting sites available for public visitation, such as some early villages near Zuni Pueblo and the site of Homolovi, which is operated by the U.S. Forest Service as a public use site in east-central Arizona.

The foregoing classification of the Anasazi peoples by geographic area is a system that archaeologists have developed to try to understand the culture. It uses a series of characteristics that are peculiar in both time and space to distinguish one group from all others. It is important to remember, however, that this is only one convenient way of viewing a culture and that other perspectives are possible and may give much better insight into the people themselves, their descendants, and the way in which their particular society and culture worked.

The system of branches of the many Anasazi groups is helpful in understanding some of the differences between the different groups, but over time, as the groups changed culturally and often from one part of the Anasazi Southwest to another, the distinctions often are blurred and sometimes confused. Current research in the area is assisting in redefinition of these branches, and in the understanding of some of the dynamics and changes that occurred between groups.

Active Archaeology

Public interest in archaeology is definitely on an upswing. For individuals with the time and interest, there are several ways to pursue archaeology. Membership in local and state archaeological societies is increasing; these societies are very active, with frequent trips to well known sites which combine backpacking and dirt road travel with a visit to backcountry archaeological resources.

In addition to trips to ruins, the groups participate in research projects with rock art, archaeological surveys, historic preservation, and, on occasion, with the excavation and analysis of specific sites.

Most states have archaeological societies that are active. It would certainly be useful to check with these local groups and find out what they do and what sort of membership they have. These groups are also a great source of information about nearby projects and activities of federal agencies, local colleges, and others that may be seeking assistance from the public.

Many local archaeological societies are also a source of training. In Colorado, for example, the Office of the State Archaeologist maintains a training program in various archaeological areas and research methods, including the ethics of conservation archaeology. This program has been training members of the Colorado Archaeological Society since the early 1980s. They are also an avenue for involvement with the community of academic, federal, state, and private archaeologists. Some of these groups need part-time field assistants and pay modest wages.

In the West and especially in the Four Corners area, the U.S. Forest Service sponsors an active, interesting volunteer program each summer. Volunteers survey archaeological and historic sites or work on archaeological and historic preservation projects such as the stabilization of sites on forest lands.

The National Park Service has a similar program called Volunteers in the Parks (VIPs). Volunteers work in parks and monuments throughout the nation in a variety of projects such as archaeology and historic preservation. These positions also involve museum curation and on-site interpretation of archaeological and historic resources.

Neither the Forest Service nor Park Service programs provide a salary, but the agencies do pay for lunches, car expenses, and sometimes housing. These programs offer an opportunity to work in archaeology for a summer or other short periods of time. They are delightful ways to spend a fascinating and worthwhile summer.

Several years ago, Northwestern University began an experiment involving the public in archaeological research at Campusville, Illinois. Instead of using the traditional college student labor for excavation at the site, adults, high school, and even junior high students performed field and laboratory activities. The program was a remarkable success. People from all over the nation, of all ages and all backgrounds, have taken part and supported the research both by their work and through the fees they pay to the program.

In the early 1980s the program was expanded to include the Crow Canyon Archaeological Center in southwestern Colorado. Crow Canyon draws hundreds of people each year to assist in excavating a large, late Pueblo III site called Sand Canyon Pueblo. The site is somewhat typical of other late Hovenweep canyon head sites that seem to represent the final Anasazi occupation in southwestern Colorado.

The center has a modern laboratory, overnight accommodations, and meal facilities. The excavations are supervised by a permanent staff of professional archaeologists, and the research is guided by a committee of respected archaeologists from throughout the nation. A fee is charged for attendance at Crow Canyon to cover room and board, tuition, and other costs.

This description of the Anasazi is only an introduction to the sites and the people who lived in them from 700 to more than 2,000 years ago. Perhaps it is a beginning, leading to an increased understanding for those fortunate enough to hike the canyons and mesas of the Four Corners.

It is hoped that as you visit ruins and increase your appreciation for early southwestern people that you will aid in the effort to preserve the sites and the artifacts that are found on them. If they continue to suffer from vandals and an uncaring public, there will almost certainly be little left for future generations in the backcountry of the Four Corners.

Acknowledgments

SCOTT WARREN: Anasazi sites have offered me an infinite array of creative possibilities and have occupied endless hours of my time. In seeing this body of work through to culmination in book form, I wish to thank first of all Northland's editor-in-chief, Susan McDonald. Without her initial and continued support, the presentation of these images would not be possible. I also want to acknowledge the "other half" of this project, Gary Matlock. From the day I wandered into his office and asked if he wanted to write a book to the day it actually ran off the press, Gary's knowledge and commitment to presenting this information in a fresh and interesting manner has added greatly to the book's quality.

Because of her faith in my abilities and her unwavering support, Beth, my wife, helped me through moments of doubt as no one else could. My mother and father also have my deep appreciation for the life they gave me and the freedom they afforded me in choosing my own path.

To two individuals who displayed patience as I sought these images, Rockford Smith and Dave Schmidt, a warm expression of gratitude is due. Perhaps we can get away for yet another slickrock canyon sojourn some day. And, to Jeremiah, my friend always—your faithful accompaniment will be a lasting memory.

With the hope that this book will further our appreciation of southwestern prehistory, I dedicate my portion to the preservation of the nation's irreplaceable antiquities.

GARY MATLOCK: Foremost among those who should be acknowledged are the many archaeologists whose research and publications provided the information contained herein. A book of this nature precludes complete bibliographic citing of all the individual research and synthetic pieces that further a general work of this nature. They are collectively a serious group of scholars and scientists who, although generally critical and occasionally quarrelsome, are a most gregarious and enjoyable group and a pleasure to work with.

Many others have helped more directly with the production and final form of this book. Scott Warren was the general instigator and often the motivating force. Susan McDonald, editor-in-chief at Northland, and Rose Houk, copy editor, carefully and intelligently managed its inception and completion. They took a massive, verbose text and reduced it to something readable; other authors can appreciate the simultaneous discomfort and gratitude that good editors evoke.

A number of colleagues assisted in both the production and the critical review of the work. Dr. Philip Duke introduced me to European concepts of public involvement in archaeology and provided an invaluable alternative sounding board for many of the archaeological concepts and ideas current in southwestern United States. Max Witkind, archaeologist with the Bureau of Land Management; Dan Murphy, archaeologist and interpretive writer for the National Park Service; and Bob York, archaeologist for the San Juan National Forest reviewed and provided numerous helpful and thoughtful comments about the text and its philosophical approach.

Dr. Douglas Scott of the Midwestern Archeological Center of the National Park Service who, like Phil Duke, helped over the years with ideas and spirited debate about archaeology, the public, and their respective roles in the preservation of the past, will find himself in the text in numerous ways, to the benefit of the entire effort.

And finally, my thanks go to Ed and Jo Berger, founders of the Crow Canyon Archeological Center, for convincing me and many others that active public involvement is good for archaeology.

Suggested Readings

The following list of suggested readings provides selected examples of recent publications in archaeology on the Anasazi and other topics discussed or specifically referred to in this book. The literature on the Anasazi is much too voluminous to attempt to cite all of the individual references drawn on in the preparation of the manuscript. Most of these readings have good bibliographies and can serve as a basis to provide a more in depth pursuit of any of the topics discussed. We have attempted to list more recent works rather than some of the older standard literature on the Anasazi. These older works will be found in the bibliographies of the books included here.

Ambler, Richard J. 1977. *The Anasazi*. Flagstaff. Museum of Northern Arizona Press.

Breternitz, David A., Arthur H. Rohn and Elizabeth A. Morris. 1974. *Prehistoric Ceramics of the Mesa Verde Region*. Flagstaff: Northern Arizona Society of Science and Arts, Inc.

Colton, Harold S. 1953. *Potsherds: An Introduction to the Study of Prehistoric Southwestern Ceramics and Their Use and Historic Reconstruction*. Flagstaff: Northern Arizona Society of Science and Arts, Inc.

Cordell, Linda S. 1984. *Prehistory of the Southwest*. Orlando: Academic Press.

Dean, Jeffrey S. 1969. *Chronological Analysis of Tsegi Phase Sites in Northeastern Arizona*. Tucson: The University of Arizona Press. (A good discussion of late Kayenta sites in northeastern Arizona and an excellent discussion of architecture, room function, and family units.)

Dutton, Bertha. 1983. *American Indians of the Southwest*. Albuquerque: University of New Mexico Press.

Grant, Campbell. 1970. *Canyon de Chelly, Its People and Rock Art*. Tucson: University of Arizona Press.

Hayes, Alden C. 1964. *The Archeological Survey of Wetherhill Mesa: Mesa Verde National Park*. Washington D.C.: National Park Service.

Hayes, Alden C., David Brugge and W. J. Judge. 1981. *Archeological Surveys of Chaco Canyon*. Washington D.C.: National Park Service.

Lekson, Stephen H. 1984. *Great Pueblo Architecture of Chaco Canyon, New Mexico*. Albuquerque: University of New Mexico Press.

Martin, Paul S. and Fred T. Plog. 1973. *The Archaeology of Arizona: A Study of the Southwest Region*. Garden City, N.Y.: Doubleday.

Nickens, Paul R. 1981. *Pueblo III Communities in Transition: Environment and Adaptation in Johnson Canyon*. Boulder: Memoirs of the Colorado Archaeological Society, No.2.

Noble, David Grant. 1984. *New Light on the Chaco*. Santa Fe: The School of American Research Press.

————. 1980. *Ancient Ruins of the Southwest*. Flagstaff: Northland Press. (An excellent guide to the better-known sites in the Southwest.)

Powers, Robert P., William B. Gillespie and Stephen H. Lekson. 1983. *The Outlier Survey: A Regional View of Settlement in the San Juan Basin*. Albuquerque: National Park Service.

Reher, Charles A., Ed. 1977. *Settlement and Subsistence Along the Lower Chaco River:*

The CGP Survey. Albuquerque: University of New Mexico Press. (This discussion of settlement, climate, and other aspects of the Chaco culture contains excellent material on ceramic and lithic technology and analysis.)

Rohn, Arthur H. 1971. *Mug House*. Washington, D.C.: National Park Service.

———. 1987. *Anasazi Ruins of the Southwest in Color*. Albuquerque: University of New Mexico Press.

Schaafsma, Polly. 1980. *Indian Rock Art of the Southwest*. Albuquerque: University of New Mexico Press.

Schwartz, Douglas W. In Press. *Dynamics of Southwestern Prehistory*. Santa Fe: School of American Research.

Smith, Jack. 1987. *Mesas, Cliffs, and Canyons: The University of Colorado Archaeological Survey of Mesa Verde National Park*. Mesa Verde Museum Association.

Willy, Gordon R. 1966. *An Introduction to American Archaeology, Vol. 1: North and Middle America*. Englewood Cliffs, N.J.: Prentice-Hall.

Offices

to Contact

for Information on

Visiting Backcountry

Sites in the

Four Corners

NATIONAL PARK SERVICE

Mesa Verde National Park
Mesa Verde National Park, CO 81330

Hovenweep National Park
Mesa Verde National Park, CO 81330

Canyon de Chelly National Monument
P.O. Box 588
Chinle, AZ 86503

Navajo National Monument
HC71, Box 3
Tonalea, AZ 86044-9704

Wupatki National Monument
2717 N. Steve's Blvd., Suite #3
Flagstaff, AZ 86001

Chaco Culture National Historical Park
Star Rt. 4, Box 6500
Bloomfield, NM 87413

Canyonlands National Park
Moab, Utah 84532

BUREAU OF LAND MANAGEMENT

San Juan Resource Area
701 Camino del Rio
Durango, CO 81301

Farmington Resource Area
900 La Plata Hwy.
Farmington, NM 87499-4204

San Juan Resource Area
P.O. Box 7
Monticello, Utah 84535

Moab District Office
P.O. Box 970
Moab, Utah 84532

Montrose District Office
2465 S. Townsend Ave.
Montrose, CO 81401

Anasazi Heritage Center
27501 Hwy. 184
Dolores, CO 81323

NATIONAL FOREST SERVICE

San Juan National Forest
701 Camino del Rio
Durango, CO 81301

Santa Fe National Forest
1220 St. Francis Drive
Santa Fe, NM 87501

Carson National Forest
Forest Service Bldg., Box 558
Taos, NM 87571

Manti-La Sal National Forest
599 W. Price River Dr.
Price, UT 84501

TRIBAL OFFICES

Navajo Tribal Parks System
P.O. Box 308
Window Rock, AZ 86515

Ute Mountain Tribal Park
Towaoc, CO 81334

The Hopi Tribe
P.O. Box 123
Kykotsmovi, AZ 86039

Zuni Pueblo
P.O. Box 339
Zuni, NM 87327

OTHERS

The San Juan County Archaeological
    Center and Library at Salmon Ruins
Rt. 3, Box 858
Farmington, NM 87401

Edge of the Cedars State Historical Park
P.O. Box 788
Blanding, Utah 84511